The
INTERIM
REVOLUTION

How crowdsourcing, the on-demand
Gig Economy and *Teams as a Service*
are transforming business globally

Pat Lynes

WRITING MATTERS PUBLISHING

The Interim Revolution

How crowdsourcing, the on-demand *Gig Economy* and *Teams as a Service* are transforming business globally

First published in 2018

Writing Matters Publishing (UK)
info@writingmatterspublishing.com
www.writingmatterspublishing.com

Cover design: Callum Chambers
Illustrations: Andrew Priestley

ISBN 978-0-9956051-2-1

Please Note: *The Interim Revolution* is intended as information only and does not constitute specific financial, investment, taxation or legal advice unique to your situation. It is for educational purposes only.

The Author, Publisher and Resellers accept no responsibility for loss, damage or injury to persons or their belongings as a direct or indirect result of reading this book.

Please note: The following terms and phrases used throughout this book are Registered Trademarks of Patrick Lynes and Sullivan & Stanley Ltd: *Sullivan & Stanley*®, *S&S*®, *The Interim Revolution*®, *TaaS*® and *The Change Society*®.

Foreword

Marshall Goldsmith
World Renowned Leadership Coach
Harvard Institute of Coaching

The knowledge *Gig Economy* gives leaders and organisations a real opportunity to tap into a trusted workforce that will help them deliver business change.

Pat Lynes' take in *The Interim Revolution,* on where the world of knowledge work is going, presents the business world with an opportunity to transform by harnessing the power of super temps via a *Teams as a Service* approach deployed to solve business problems and deliver successful outcomes.

The book brings the sharing, collaborative and knowledge economy to life to help organisations change and form into a 21st Century operating model and prepare for the future of work.

The title of one of my books *What Got You Here, Won't Get You There* is encapsulated in what Pat Lynes' *Teams as a Service* model is bringing to the business world. Old routes to capability aren't as successful as they once were.

This is a refreshing alternative with a strong coaching underpin that I feel is a must-read for any executive looking to future-proof their organisation and career in a fast-changing world.

Testimonials for Pat Lynes, Sullivan & Stanley and The Change Society

In a business world of disruption, it seems unreal that two major supplier industries (Recruitment in all its guises and Management Consulting) continue to operate as if nothing has changed.

The author has highlighted and is indeed implementing a solution that will give organisations a quantum leap forward in terms of delivery speed and quality. As an interim of 15 years, this model makes far more sense that the one-man mercenary and light years ahead of the *'We came, We saw, We invoiced'* mantra of the consulting world.

I hope that many organisations can see the potential as the rewards are compelling.

Great read sir.

Steve Sutton, *Transformation Director*

Quite simply a must read - vision coupled with Pat's obvious passion, skill and ability to deliver. This is the future way of work.

Christian McMahon, *Top 10 Global CIO*

Sullivan & Stanley is a highly supportive community for executive Interims. Focused, innovative and tailored around solving problems for business' and CIOs. The fresh *Teams as a Service* approach to delivery and advisory is innovative, well-timed and something CIOs and organisations have found powerful and useful as an alternative to consulting companies.

Mark Chillingworth
CIO Editor, ICON Business Media

Pat Lyne's commitment, energy and vision to shaping the Interim market of the future come through strongly from the first page. His new ideas and how they will support real change in organisations makes for an exciting book. Fascinating read for anyone involved in this industry.

Jacqueline Shakespeare, *Transformation Director*

The market has been crying out for this model for many years. I think we have had enough of the big consulting firms putting in a team of expensive *juniors* with little experience around one or two competent *seniors*.

Finally, *S&S* has cracked it - a business that really does have a new model that has access to great people and is able to group a powerful, flexible workforce of Interims with the right capability to deliver - brilliant!

Malcolm Lambell, CIO

I like that my time isn't wasted anymore and that I can get the solutions I need to get great people around me, in a team spirit that delivers outcomes and solves the board pressures that face me. What I like about *Sullivan & Stanley* is their ability to swarm around problems to rectify with the least amount of pain to me.

Mark Harrison, CIO

As Head of IT at *Argos*, Patrick supported my urgent and demanding need to provide three senior Interim managers, to take ownership of critical programmes in the *Argos Transformation*. His skill in getting underneath the brief, together with his strong network, meant that I successfully appointed credible ex-IT Directors into those roles, all of whom were able to make an immediate impact and shape the success of the overall programme. His ability to tap into his network to provide credible resources quickly saved precious time and makes him my first port of call when looking for Interim management solutions.

Keith Graves
Senior Consultant, Leading Resolutions

Pat's advice and insights are invaluable. As an independent, the support network Pat has created via *Sullivan & Stanley's Change Society* community is incredible, giving me a great sense of community and support with access to a global network of expertise on pretty much any organisational topic.

Michael Condon, *Quality Management Expert*

I have used Patrick for a number of years to reliably recruit high calibre Interim consultants that many other agencies seem to struggle to find. He has a 100% record of completing the assignments I have tasked him with. This consistent quick delivery of quality verified candidates, is what really adds value and differentiates Patrick. I have found the rigorous vetting and referencing processes he puts in place, makes the real difference from the typical agency model. All of the candidates he has surrounded me with have delivered on their mandates.

Clive Phelps, *VP, Core Network Delivery*

Sullivan & Stanley helped me pull together a *Transformation Team* for a very challenging, private equity backed technology transformation mandate at *UNIT4* in Utrecht.

The assignment required six Interims to drive this delivery and within days of contact, Patrick and his team had provided a targeted selection of very strong Interim candidates for each of the six positions we needed. The speed, quality of service, and process management led by Pat helped me to deliver against a very aggressive mandate. Patrick is very personable, has excellent follow-through and I would have no hesitation in recommending him going forward.

Tim Fulton
Chief of Operations, IT Solutions, Kantar Media

Pat is an excellent recruiter. His candidate briefs are first class. His effort in ensuring there is a cultural fit before presenting a candidate clearly pay off. Every aspect of the brief is covered with the candidate so very few time wasting interviews. As well as all the help he has afforded in the recruitment process he has now placed me in two Interim CIO roles.

I would whole heartedly recommend Patrick, whose enthusiasm and ability to understand the cultural and technical requirements of many varied organizations has also rubbed off on his team who I have also found to be first class.

James Hendry, *CIO*

An honest and forward-thinking view of the executive, technical and programme management side of the Gig Economy. Perfect to dip into for tips, or a slow, deep read and reflection.

A book that asks some challenging questions of an industry sector that has for far too long failed to deliver and not kept up with the demands of their clients. May be a disturbing read for some. A breath of fresh air to this reader.

Peter O'Rourke, *CIO*

I've been lucky enough to meet Pat in my own journey from executive life to the gig economy. This man has a vision, and he also has the energy and skills to put that into practise. This book tells you, in one clear easy read, all you need to know about why he's doing what he does, what he believes needs to change and how he's going about delivering that change.

Adrian Wakefield, *CIO*

A great read if you are tired with the stale, old models for finding talent, and want to hear about something new and disruptive. The articulation of the current problems with the market really resonated with my own experiences.

Recommended for anyone trying to affect change in organisations.

Adrian Stalham, *Transformation Director*

Extremely insightful and totally credible - Pat clearly has a thorough understanding of his subject from a practical, real-life perspective. Read through it in one session and found several "moments of clarity" where Pat phrased things in crystal clarity! Must-read for anyone involved, or considering becoming or using interim solutions.

Chris Davis, *Transformation Director*

A must read for anybody who is looking for an alternative to big Consultancies. This book provides an alternative approach through the use of experienced Interims and resonates with what I have seen in the market over the past 15 years. This is a great read.

Nick Powell, *Senior Change Agent*

I've known Pat for five years and continue to be delighted and surprised by the quality of his network and follow through.

Pat has placed me at *Warner*, provided interviews for me at *Burberry, Apple* and now a consulting role at *Liverpool FC*, which is my dream assignment. The calibre of those brands are testament to the quality of service Pat has brought into a crowded tired market; people want to work with him.

Pat is, without doubt, one of the best Interim partners I've met and he has an exceptional network. His new *Teams* model is disrupting old outdated approaches to recruitment and consulting which is very much needed in both industries.

Highly recommended.

Mitul Patel
Programme Director at Liverpool FC

Being introduced to *Sullivan & Stanley, The Change Society* and Pat Lynes has been great. Great people, an abundance of opportunity and potentially one of the first companies to genuinely crack the emerging hybrid recruitment/consulting market properly.

Colin Wilson, *Technology Leader*

Dedication

This book is dedicated to my two sons, Sullivan and Stanley, who bring so much joy into my life. The inspiration for this book and my challenger company is to inspire the future of work for their generation.

Contents

At a glance

Individuals

The traditional solution for companies who require expert input is to temporarily engage individual expert Interims iteratively.

Disruptive Technology and Rapid Change

But technology innovations now come so fast they have become *the* significant global disruptive force and the biggest challenge for large companies who lack the capability, speed and agility to respond to rapid change.

Teams as a Service

As a result there has been a paradigm shift from placing individuals, to placing teams. The future is pre-formed, pre-gelled teams.

The Hollywood Model

Think Hollywood. Think box-office success.

Hollywood studios rarely employ production staff. Hollywood producers now assemble teams of the top 5% of talent for the life of that movie project. Once finished, the teams disperse.

In essence, this is an obvious example of the *Gig Economy*.

Pat Lynes, *Global Recruiter of the Year 2015,* now knows the power of assembling top 5% expert Interim teams. Teams of expert Interims are not the future - they are a reality, now.

Sullivan & Stanley

Pat left a senior position at a leading traditional independent recruitment agency to start his company, *Sullivan & Stanley,* and to pioneer a radical new approach called *Teams as a Service (TaaS).*

The essence of the *Teams as a Service (TaaS)* model is pre-gelled top 5% executive Interim teams. Subsequently, *Sullivan & Stanley* are at the forefront of the booming *Executive Gig Economy.*

The Interim Revolution

The Interim Revolution explains crowd-sourcing, the *Gig Economy* (with a focus on the top 5% of executive Interims), expert communities and *Teams as a Service.*

The Interim Revolution

Named client case studies used in this book are used with permission of the clients. Other case studies have been anonymised to honour client confidentiality.

Pat Lynes and Sullivan & Stanley

The author, Pat Lynes was *Global Interim Recruiter of the Year 2015* and is the Founder and CEO of *Sullivan & Stanley,* a fast growing, international expert Interim hub, based in London.

They can be contacted via:

TIR@sullivanstanley.com
www.sullivanstanley.com

The Interim Revolution:
Introduction

Do you remember *Blockbuster*?

Remember how you used to go down to *Blockbuster* on a Friday and rent the latest DVDs? *Blockbuster* was the number one DVD franchise organisation on the planet. But then it went bankrupt. *Blockbuster* missed the technology trend – online streaming; it didn't listen to their customers and even turned down a partnership with *Netflix* – today worth USD$28 billion.

In short, they resisted change and when they finally realised the reality and pace of the emerging trend, they failed to respond quickly enough. The result was *Blockbuster* went into bankruptcy.

Understand, change is not *a thing*. Change doesn't have a deadline. It is ongoing, perpetual and happening right now - with or without you or your organisation.

And more and more, emergent change is disrupting the very essence of the enterprise at a *rapid* pace.

Some companies look inward to meet this challenge but more and more companies are utilising outside professionals – expert Interims – to drive solutions and transformation.

My business, *Sullivan & Stanley*, specialises in connecting Interim professionals to established companies that have to embrace rapid change. Right now.

Fresh models are needed to embrace such change.

Individual or isolated Interim appointments has been the traditional response.

But individuals cannot cope with the demands of such rapid change. *Teams can.*

This book sets out to define such a model using pre-gelled, top 5%, A-grade, teams of Interims – i.e., executive freelancers who work independently and can be deployed on demand.

Working with two of the UK's best known recruitment firms, I've been placing Interims for over 15 years. I have resourced over 100 successful transformations for the likes of *Burberry, Argos* and *Sky* and in 2015 won *Global Interim Recruiter of the Year.*

In 2016, I became disillusioned with what I felt was a tired recruitment model, left my long term employer and started *Sullivan & Stanley* to focus on the *Teams as a Service* model. In just over a year, we grew into a healthy, high-growth business delivering the *Teams as a Service* model *(TaaS).*

Like most businesses, mine was borne from noticing problems that needed fixing in order to help organisations deliver faster and move quickly at scale.

Having interviewed 100 executives, I discovered three key problems in the recruitment and consultancy market, which demonstrated that existing models were failing.

Companies don't have:

1. *The calibre of people they need in order to change*
2. *The agility to change i.e., they can't move quickly enough as they're sitting in old organisational designs that no longer serve them*
3. *Effective routes to capability via their current recruiters and consultancies*

This has created a *capability* and *speed* gap that is widening daily.

Specifically, technology has changed the game. Newer faster disruptive businesses are grabbing market share and, consequently, constant change has become the new norm. Yet most larger companies are woefully unprepared.

Enter *The Interim Revolution*. *The Interim Revolution* is essentially using freelance, high calibre professionals on short or long term, temporary appointments called *gigs*, to assist with solving business problems and major change projects such as IT, culture change, organisational development and so on.

And the *Gig Economy* is growing. I strongly believe that using Interims is now a cost-effective, bona fide way of solving these business problems, so I'm on a mission to create a crowd company powered by the Interim crowd to help the business world evolve.

As such, I've identified a gap in the market which sits in-between recruitment and consulting models.

My spin on this is simple. I have pivoted from the traditional model - placing individuals; to placing teams with clients.

Trusted, high-calibre, flexible teams for hire can offer all the knowledge and problem-solving skills you need, how you want it and when you want it.

Hollywood and Teams as a Service

I've taken inspiration from the Hollywood production model, where directors handpick the best creative and technical people for their production.

With this in mind - I've created a four-step *Teams as a Service (TaaS)* model that follows a similar process but with business executives.

This starts with a personalised discovery session with clients to flesh out the mission, before casting and gelling the team that we then deploy with the client to deliver rapid results.

In this way, the recruiter acts as the *Casting Director* and the Interim Partner directs and leads the production with the executives.

Interim *Teams as a Service (TaaS)* brings the Hollywood model to life in the business world to help our clients transform.

I believe there is an incredible company at the intersection of recruiters and independent Interims and it's an idea I've had in my head for years. I believe in it so much that I left a secure, well-paid executive role with a recruitment company I co-built to bring this concept to life.

So, my new big game is to build a global change partner powered by the Interim crowd, with a core purpose of working with organisations to give them a change capability.

The Change Society

As a result, I have created a *Change Society* community, made up of hundreds of associates and Interim partners ready to be deployed. We've already won a consulting project to transform an institutionalised financial services organisation into a product-based Fintech model, which we won against one of the *Big Four* consulting firms.

This is just the start of the revolution.

The *Gig Economy* is on the rise and statistics suggest around 50% of the US and European workforce will be freelance by 2020.

As the talent drain into the *Gig Economy* explodes, our teams concept is nicely poised to transform older companies into new ones and help them avoid becoming the next *Blockbuster*.

Introduction: The Story So Far

In order to know where I'm coming from, you ought to know a little more about where I've come from.

For, if I am going to start a revolution, if you are going to join me on my quest, I'm going to need to inspire you to act, and I can't do that unless you know my 'why'. The reason behind the revolution, *the why* behind the mission, that inspires action.

As Simon Sinek says in *Start With Why*, "People don't buy what you do, they buy why you do it."

As a specialist technology and change Interim recruiter, I deal with organisations looking to transform their business through technology. So I deliver the glue that surrounds such projects. This may involve adding a board member, a mid-market manager, or an Interim CIO or CTO leader. It always involves sourcing the best quality knowledge workers, change agents and Interim leaders I can find within the communities I've spent the past 15 years building.

Communities for whom I've been sufficiently responsive with opportunities. Because communities, like people, matter.

"Always surround yourself with great people, son!"
Diarmuid Lynes, Retired CEO of global banking corporation

My early memories of communities are people smiling and helping each other out. Born on the 16th November 1978 to two Irish immigrants who were keen to build a community in their new neighbourhood, I was brought up in the Woodford Green area of London within a thriving Irish/English community and schooled with a group a friends who I still call my best mates today. My father is a staunch Catholic and a member of the Catenian society and I recall my family frequently attending events, church and golf days.

From an early age, two pieces of my father's advice have been ingrained in my mind:

"Treat people like you would expect to be treated yourself."

"You have to surround yourself with great people."

My father joined a bank in 1973 where he started in Dublin as a porter, licking stamps and performing administration tasks.

His hard-work ethic and natural affinity with people saw him rise through the ranks, until he was promoted to Assistant Manager of the Holloway Road branch in Islington, North London, and the Lynes English dynasty began.

Shortly afterwards, dad became Branch Manager and I remember his sense of teamwork and community shining through all that he did.

I always fondly remember walking into local shops and restaurants and noticing how my father was treated like royalty by the shop and business owners he lent money to.

He would always take the time to look them in the eye and get to know each customer individually. He'd learn as much as he could about their family, background, environment and their general ways before lending; and after, ways to help them pursue and grow their business ventures. As a result, dad was part of the heart of the community, and by default, so was I.

This feeling of being part of a community stayed with me.

It was all about connection. It was all about providing a personalised service around customer needs, getting out to see people and building career-lasting relationships for the longer-term - a core value of mine.

Over the years, my father also enjoyed some downtime with the people he surrounded himself with. Every year the infamous Lynes' summer BBQ would be quite the event. 80 Irish people shipped out from London in coaches to feast on cooked meats and have a good old knees-up.

It was also my first brush with *entrepreneurship.*

I quickly figured out the Irish folk were very generous with their money. I used to pocket a good £70-£200 per BBQ from the generous congregation.

The family atmosphere my father built in his branches has etched itself in my memory. This community vibe continued throughout his 15-year stint as an offshore CEO for the same bank, where he ran a large banking operation.

As CEO, his mantra remained the same as when he was licking stamps: *surround yourself with great people.*

After all, business life is tough enough, right?

He always used to hand-pick his players to lead the business to victorious success, and this has always been a core value of mine, ever since I first entered the recruitment industry.

Indeed, community building and recruitment were a glove fit for me.

Community Building, Personalisation and Aligned Match-Making

In fact, my whole career has been built out of creating networks to resolve a need.

Back in 1999, I co-built a community-based website for DJs, promoters, record label bosses and fans.

My first step into community building actually started with a *house and trance* website where I would generate performance gigs for DJs, myself included, and connect up-and-coming DJs to *gig* opportunities.

I built a network to connect up-and-coming DJs to gigs with established promoters, dance organisations and clubs.

The site was content driven around reviews of club nights, promotions, record labels, and DJs of the month. We had a sufficiently addictive chat board.

Back in 2000, our chat forum and website network would fill with like-minded people, chatting about gigs, records, nights out, and so on. I had mixed this community of promoters, record label owners, producers, and DJs.

One day, Europe's largest dance promoter booked our *DJ of the month*. As a result, the site took off and the opportunities spiralled. The DJs listed on the site, myself included, ended up DJ-ing all around Europe and we became the hottest website for that genre of music in Europe.

I was connecting people to opportunities, right back when I was 18. And this is why I felt I had truly found my calling with recruitment. I get so much pleasure from finding people opportunities and jobs, whether it's a DJ gig or a change management gig.

So, you could say, I've been working in the *Gig Economy* long before the *Gig Economy* became a legitimate term.

These days, I'm doing the grown-up version of this by placing people into boards to change companies. I'm still generating gigs, albeit for executives and knowledge workers in a booming *Executive Gig Economy*.

What I'm doing now is an extension of what I did then.

Community first

Today I recruit leaders, teams and change agents for companies who need knowledge, leadership and delivery for hire.

As such, community first, commerce second has been a real thread of my career.

Earlier in my career, I built a telecoms division from scratch, building communities of *Cisco* engineers, architects and project managers.

More recently, I built a high performing contracts/Interim business; teaching the business of 100+ people how to build a community, cultivate a tribe, become a topic expert and add value as a recruiter, which, I'm proud to say, is still their core strategy for developing recruiters today.

Interim means a lot of different things for different people, from freelancer to contractor. But, for the purposes of this book we'll use the word *Interim* as a cover-all term for *contracted knowledge worker.*

Throughout this time, I've spent a lot of time talking to people - agency, consultancy and client side - to tap into what the future might hold. To uncover what companies want and need. And to find out what I might do to help, influence and shape the world of recruitment for the future generation.

Revolutionising recruitment matters so much to me because people matter in business. And this is why I left the security of a well-paid equity holding role at a respected recruitment agency to pioneer a new model that has the potential to turn this established but tired industry on its head. It was a case of *what if?* and *why not?* What if I don't do something and someone else does, and why not at least try?

So I resigned and gave myself the space I needed to create a fresh model for the next generation of industry and developed a composite model which I tested in the market.

During that time I spoke to 100 executives working within the industry and gathered sufficient industry data.

This book is the result of my research and development of the *Teams as a Service* model.

It's a book that I've written to demonstrate a fresh way to deliver certainty in an uncertain age; a new way to challenge organisations to reinvent their traditional core, which is not limited to satisfying the needs of the shareholders driven by short-termism in the *C-Suite*.

Essentially, I want to challenge corporate thinking and provide a better way that can revolutionise recruitment and consulting services.

It's a book for *C-Suite* directors of growing and established corporations. It's a book for executives who want a different relationship with their work. It's a book about transforming *organisational, technological* and *people debt* into *capability credit*, by allowing a trusted partner to provide you with agility that will bolster your ability.

However, this book is not a guide. It's a book which aims to help you make sense of what is happening right now. It's a book which delivers a fresh framework and model to use to boost your company's health and deliver transformation. It's a book that explores how doing so is possible by surrounding yourself with great people and teams, all equipped to face the changing landscape head on.

I hope you enjoy reading it and are sufficiently inspired to make the right changes for your career and company.

Pat Lynes

Chapter 1

Why a Revolutionary Recruitment and Consulting Model is Needed

Chapter 1: Why a Revolutionary Recruitment and Consulting Model is Needed

"What got you here, won't get you there."
Marshall Goldsmith
World Renowned Leadership Coach

Different ways of working are unfolding amid an economic climate of uncertainty and constant change. Year on year, the rate of technological advancement increases; day by day, the capability gap and speed gap widen.

And all the while, a war for talent rages on.

Today, more than ever before, organisations need to be *agile* and deliver fast, if they are to exceed expectations and optimise operations in an increasingly complex world.

But the rapidly widening *capability gap* makes meeting those imperatives difficult. These complex challenges are demanding that organisations think differently and consider new, relevant practices, rather than hold on to past practices that are failing to deliver. It is mission critical for them to do so.

Sadly, most aren't prepared for such seismic change.

Such seismic transformation requires a completely different mindset and different partnership model, where value, agility and sustainability are prioritised. The simple fact is, within a constantly changing climate, methods that used to work, no longer do.

Change is the new normal now

This rapid pace of change, high level of uncertainty and the threat of volatility are the lexicon of today's corporate landscape. One that has grown in complexity as a result of a perfect storm of economic, social, political and technological changes over the past few years; a perfect storm of change created by digital disruption, the network economy and different ways of working.

This has created a tremendous shift away from a *closed* and *controlled* landscape towards an *open* and *collaborative* one.

Across many industries, starting with the financial one, trust has eroded and uncertainty exploded.

Primarily, *digital disruption* has caught out the more established players and driven the *speed gap*.

Where the 20th century corporation focused on efficient production using labour and capital, the 21st century corporation co-creates and innovates at pace using knowledge networks and a fusion of entrepreneurship and intrapreneurship.

Peter Drucker accurately predicted that there would be a shift to a *knowledge society* when he wrote about regular periods of transformation back in 1992.

Indeed, he was advocating the autonomy of decision-making and accountability throughout organisations back in 1954; just as he was advocating the engagement and motivation of people through providing a sense of purpose.

He knew then that, if business leaders didn't move with these shifts; gaps in capability, performance and agility would widen. Consequently, companies would take on more than they could deliver and fail to meet expectations.

So here we are, in a business landscape of perpetual change, where it's not easy to keep up, let alone stay ahead.

As the business landscape shifts in this way, and as key talent chooses to have a different relationship with their work; the challenge facing today's enterprises is to change their operating models to be faster and more responsive, so they can pivot as needed and required.

This need for speed and agility becomes all the more vital as new well-funded start-ups, designed with agility at the core, bring highly disruptive models to the market with no technical or organisational debt.

Pure digital start-ups and newer businesses are more agile by default, having been designed from the ground up, which makes pivoting far easier. For older corporations, pivoting is less easy. They have legacy technology and organisational debt which means embracing digital disruption is not something that can be done quickly or easily. And yet change they must.

Indeed as Dan Priestley says in his book, *Key Person of Influence:*

> *"Your best thinking from three years ago,*
> *is your biggest baggage today."*

While the *Responsive.org Manifesto* defines this further:

> *"The tension between organisations optimised for*
> *predictability and the unpredictable world they inhabit*
> *has reached a breaking point."*

Here's what we know for sure. The old world is dying and the new world is happening.

The collision of these worlds is causing chaos and complexity in business. Models that we had grown accustomed to die out or, as is the case with the consultancy model, become a false economy.

If you haven't noticed, this includes the recruitment model.

Consequently, boards, CIOs and CTOs are facing increasing pressures, enhanced by the widening capability and speed gaps and resulting organisational and technical debt. And, without the right trusted partners, they struggle to get to where they need to be and go out of business, as the industrial and disruptive world collide.

The only way forward is to consider and try something fresh. We have no other choice than to think differently and act accordingly because past practices are increasingly no longer fit-for-purpose. From our perspective, unless corporates make changes around how they source people and try new models, these capability and speed gaps will widen and overcome them, swallowing them up.

Unfortunately most organisations don't have the capability or agility to adapt.

They are sitting within organisational structures that were fit for the nineties and maybe the noughties, but aren't fit for today's rapid-pace, changing world. Transformation for many is no longer a choice.

Indeed, for some, change is too rapid to know where to start the transformation.

Many find it hard balancing today's demands, including simply keeping the lights on and the estate running, with tomorrow's essentials along with a punishing innovation agenda.

Some fear change and would rather play it safe.

CEOs have a board to address. Keeping shareholders happy whilst maintaining personal ambition, bonus payments and safeguarding the certainty of a good career, add to this fear. The easiest option for the CEO in this instance is *not* to rock the boat, but instead to seek the comfort of targets and rigid plans.

We now know that this aversion to changing plans slows down response rates and stifles creativity, but, frankly, this is often of less importance to the comfort-zone-friendly-CEO than the security of his or her career and maintaining the status quo (and board remuneration) for shareholders. As such, fear leads many leaders to take the easy route, as does the *if it ain't broke, don't fix it, cost before value* and *but it worked here last year* mentality.

However, this is a false economy.

Stifled creativity and slower productivity will eventually impact the bottom line and leave shareholders scratching their heads.

By contrast, delivering change effectively will future-proof the organisation.

Given that access to the top five per cent of global talent is now within reach, you'd think that leaders might be reassured. Yet, sadly, many respond by burying their heads in their sand. But those who do, lose them. And so the whirlwind sucks them up into its vortex and spits them out sometime later, bewildered – their best people gone, their resources less human and their culture shocked.

"We always overestimate the change that will occur in the next two years and underestimate the change that will occur in the next ten. Don't let yourself be lulled into inaction."
Bill Gates, *Microsoft Founder*

Conversely, newer organisations are in a constant state of transformation, pivoting more readily than organisations limited by legacy leadership and old operating models; moving closer towards the bullseye of what the customer and internal clients want. Such companies enable themselves to be agile at scale by assembling (and reassembling) themselves into groups of better-performing networks.

Such companies have discovered a better way that embraces the emergent shifts driving this new business landscape. A way that prioritises people and enables flexibility.

But for established players, being agile enough to change is not easy. We know that change is tough.

The majority of respondents in a recent *Gartner* survey (2016) (59%) said their companies were unprepared to meet the digital age within the next two years.

Hence, change programmes frequently remain unfinished, take far longer and cost way more than planned with, and according to the *University of Oxford*, only 16% reaching their objectives.

It's a statistic that I believe is fairly accurate from my insights into the industry. Given the sheer size of organisational and technical debt that most CIOs and businesses are facing, it's no surprise that organisations are finding it so hard to be agile at scale due to their size and perceived inability to restructure efficiently.

Hence why a fresh approach is needed.

Studies have shown that, in order to overcome these obstacles to successful change management, it's no good to simply pay lip service to encouraging innovation, rather we need to enable collaboration across internal and external boundaries and tap into the wealth of diverse knowledge and experience that is now available to us.

Essentially, we need to develop different ways of working and cultures that actually facilitate the generation of new ideas and strategic problem-solving.

One way to achieve this and flourish rather than languish amid uncertainty, is to consider how and who you hire; and to focus on matching the right people for the right challenges at the right time.

And that is what this book is all about.

During my 15 years in the recruitment business and having interviewed over 100 *C-Suite* executives, I have uncovered better practices that are suited to this new ever-changing world. These practices involve hiring agile teams, using Interim management and aligning processes, people and partners to create certainty in an uncertain climate.

I have discovered that successful change isn't just about surrounding yourself with the best people; it's about surrounding yourself with the best *collection of people*: the *best teams.*

The good news is, today it is possible to tap into the power of the collective mind of external in-demand experts on-demand. You just need to know where to find them. Which is where we come in.

This book explores how to do this effectively.

How We Deal With Change Really Matters

It is clear to see why leaders and boards do shy away from big changes. Striving to innovate and grow and become more agile and flexible is not an easy undertaking. Some boat-rocking could well happen as a result of change and business leaders with a board to answer to are not often keen to do that.

The proven approach is all about taking smaller steps, trialling a small teams approach to delivering success, which enables business leaders to celebrate that at board/executive level.

A central question that needs to be answered is: "How do I gain delivery predictability, hire/retain the right people, whilst managing change effectively and keeping the board happy?"

Sullivan & Stanley and *The Change Society* movement aims to answer this question and deliver a solution that even the most change-averse *C-Suite* executives will be able to embrace.

The *Teams as a Service* model we have developed helps close the *capability* and *rate of change* gap via *A-Teams* of Interim talent and by delivering in small fast-paced iterations.

Isolated Interims really can no longer solve the problem of rapid change/rapid transformation, but teams of Interims can. I aim to demonstrate the power of a team of Interims in winning the war on talent and helping organisations drive more simplistic models so they can deliver faster and move quickly at scale.

Being The Change

"Don't complain; contribute."
Simon Sinek

People make the difference, true. But I believe that the *right teams* of the *right people* make the difference in business; and that *diverse teams* are the future.

A growing awareness that placing individual Interims was an insufficient solution led me to creating a new model of successfully trialling the placement of pre-gelled freelance teams of expert Interims.

Yet, rather than merely wax lyrical about my beliefs, I decided that, in order to make a difference, I needed to, as Ghandi suggested, "Be the change I wanted to see in the world".

Disruptive ideas occur within markets where there are many unsatisfied customers. And, I'm sure you'll agree, the recruitment and consulting industry is ready for a disruptive idea to shake things up.

The *Teams as a Service* model was borne out of an awareness and frustration that individual placements weren't as effective and too unstructured for coping with rapid change; and a growing unrest in the recruitment and consultancy market.

Having worked agency-side for almost two decades I began to notice mistakes being made in the wider recruitment and consulting industry that weren't helping clients nor candidates.

Rather, there appeared to be a *race-to-the-bottom* and a *broken-value exchange* for the whole eco-system; from client to candidate and back again.

I had been a board director of a successful technology and change recruitment company, which I built over six years with the founder. I'd noticed that the rest of the industry seemed to be in a massive rush to commoditise the provision of people. Only a few companies, such as ours, seemed unwilling to become commodity players.

Yet this noticeable shift meant there was widespread and growing dissatisfaction within the marketplace as more and more clients perceived their expectations were consistently failing to be met and they felt they were being under-served.

What I love about my industry is the interaction with people, the building of networks and the matching of opportunities with talent to make a real difference. Yet, in the wider industry, I was seeing a real seismic shift towards removing that control from the recruiter.

That just didn't feel right. When you love what you do, you notice when the industry that you operate in changes.

The frustration in the recruitment and consulting field was rising as the value exchange continued to falter.

Companies needing recruitment help became increasingly over-processed and bloated as they prioritised cost over value and subsequently suffered the consequences. I was witnessing the unspoken truth of in-experienced recruitment partners and interview burden. Simultaneously, my drive to do something about it was growing.

In my previous role, I truly believed in their mission to treat candidates with the utmost best service care in the industry. I still do. I felt proud to work for companies that looked after its candidates in this way, and was pleased with what I had helped build. Yet my role was becoming more operational and I'm not a full-time ops guy.

I love building stuff and proving models and I felt there was a better way generally for the industry-at-large.

My entrepreneurial spirit and my observations about the wider dissatisfaction within the industry (which we'll explore in *Chapter 3*) were bubbling away and I knew needed to get out there and *be the change I wanted to see in the world*.

What I was seeing in the industry was such a powerful draw. The market was dictating it.

And, after building a successful recruitment company and winning *Global Interim Recruiter of the Year* by a major institute body, I felt I now had the confidence and smarts to make an impact. Every part of my being was saying I needed to step up to the challenge, leave my role as board director and go out and give myself time to find and develop a market solution.

Only then would I be able to embark on a venture where I could make a difference.

I believe there are three key phases to *being that difference*.

THE INTERIM REVOLUTION

Phase 1
Discovering and Uncovering the Problems

The real notable problem in the market is trying to find great people at scale. It's difficult to find a partner who you can trust.

On one side, you've got the lottery of recruitment agencies and the interview burden they put your organisation under. On the other side, you've got the faltering trust in management consultancies that has arisen from years of their failing to meet expectations.

Additionally there is a notable *lack of planning.*

Poor front-end decisions are being made with sourcing and consulting choices due to an obsession with cost-saving, but the cost of wrong hires is far higher than any saving, creating a false economy.

There is strategic misalignment at board level and between senior leadership teams, partners, and client needs.

All of this causes companies to hire reactively, under a state of duress, rather than proactively.

And, rather than solve the problem and add value, recruiters are (and still are) compounding the problems.

My defining moment came in 2015 when I attended a *Deloitte Recruitment Index Forum.*

The CEO of *APSCo* closed the afternoon by warning 100 recruitment directors and business owners that disruption was coming to our industry.

Her advice was that the future recruiters who adapt and thrive will be those who do the following:

- *Embed themselves in their client board's business plan*
- *Consistently explore ways to build more value around their processes and service offerings*

I couldn't have agreed more with her and hadn't witnessed many external recruiters who are a part of any boards plan or who are doing anything other than *body-shopping* and CV sifting.

And so began my journey into inquiring amongst my network about the disruptive possibilities within the future of recruitment and consulting.

Over many months, I'd awoken each morning and thought to myself, *'What would Branson do?'*

I admire Sir Richard Branson because he is renowned for successfully shaking up traditional or tired industries and my industry is definitely overdue for a shake-up.

I wondered, *'How can I make a dent in the world to actually influence some positive change here? How can I challenge existing alternatives to drastically improve the traditional recruitment and consulting model?'*

So, I set about considering what *that* might look like and how I could bring that fresh model to market. How might I use my expertise around building networks of high performing Interim change leaders?

The key questions appear to be:

- *What is it that the market wants/needs?*
- *What is missing?*
- *What new model would help organisations capitalise on the rise of the flexible economy?*
- *How can I help corporates get it right when it comes to people?*

All fairly challenging, but my daily morning juice. And it wasn't long before I discovered suitable answers.

I already knew that value, trust, alignment and customer obsession were missing.

I decided to embark on a project to interview 100 influential *C-Suite* executives and senior change agents to document their views.

I asked these executives – both client and candidate side - about their goals and how a new framework might help them to achieve those goals.

Because, in order to redefine recruitment and the provision of advisory and trusted consulting, I needed to uncover the core issues and develop a game-changing solution. One that would fill the gap in the current market, solve the problems being faced on a daily basis and enable businesses to thrive, by giving them a process to mobilise knowledge workers quickly, while improving internal capability.

In *Chapter 3*, you'll read a detailed account of the key mistakes and problems that those interviewees flagged up, with industry reports and market commentary backed-up.

The core issue though was clear: what's out there at the moment isn't working for clients, isn't working for candidates and doesn't work for great recruiters.

It was time for a change, time to challenge the status quo, time to shake things up.

My view that the *capability* and *speed* gap is widening daily was shared and corroborated by 85% of the executives contacted.

It was further substantiated by the wider community, academic articles and market research; from *Gartner (2009)* and *IBM/Forrester* research (2016); to *CIO Magazine*.

For example, according to *CIO Magazine*, *'despite today's much trumpeted technical and digital skill gaps, the big IT capability gap is still in leadership and people management capability.'*

While, the *Gartner* study (2009) shows that CIOs ranked *'improving business processes'* as their number one business priority, in reality, since that survey, processes around recruiting people have caused the gaps to widen rather than shrink.

As well as speaking directly to those affected by the mistakes being made and repeated industry-wide, I explored the world of work and enterprise to uncover how changes abound were impacting the industry further.

Phase 2
Trend-Spotting

The trend for excellent people coming in to their prime and wanting a different relationship with their work is prevailing.

People at the top of their professions are coming to me in droves, telling me they would like to be released from the shackles of politics, of functional management, of payrolling, of updating details on SAP, of appraisals ... and so on.

The corporate ladder dream is dying and people *are* voting with their feet.

They want to use their IP. They want to maximise their strengths and abilities. They want to be pro-active. They want to use their experience, their scar tissue, and harness their polished way of doing things on an Interim basis.

Doing so gives them the opportunity to focus on delivering an objective; delivering something of real value; and getting the passion back into their work.

The traditional relationship between employer and employee *is* shifting. Rapidly. Let me explain.

Top quality executives are now favouring the option to work with more than one employer, either by taking on freelance gigs that flow back-to-back, by taking on consultancy roles, working in an advisory and Interim capacity simultaneously, as well as other executive portfolio activities, like investing, taking on *Non-Executive-Directorships*, and so on.

This sits well alongside the well-documented rise of the

Gig Economy which is seeing more and more talented people leaving the shackles of full time work to use their intellectual capital in a different place at a different pace.

I noticed that *flexibility* and *agility* have become buzz words. And control over *work-life balance* has become the driving force.

Moreover, clients seem happy with this change. Here's why.

It enables them to cast a wider net to secure a more effective breadth of top talent from a pool of people they would not have been able to afford to hire in a full time capacity.

It also provides the dual benefit of both a value-added and cost-effective solution.

Given the mounting pressure to deliver increased efficiency, rather than pay people a fixed salary, why not pay people when they provide an answer to a problem or solution to a series of problems?

Furthermore, candidates report feeling more engaged in this Interim flexible world of work and clients report improved results from hiring the best of the best; people who are focused during the project period, who then leave much of their knowledge behind with the permanent staff.

This is being recognised as a more powerful way to tap into talent and get the most from that talent for your incumbent permanent talent.

True talent optimisation.

I quickly realised that this trend should be encouraged. For this is a way to enable and empower great people in their prime to make a difference, manage change and maximise their effectiveness, and likewise, enable and empower companies to thrive.

As the pace of business and change increased, so did the speed of movement *away from* centralisation towards a more decentralised world, where products and services were being *pulled* rather than *pushed*. Through my research, I was seeing shifts towards more agile and responsive autonomous cultures and processes. This enabled volatility and uncertainty to be better governed.

The *crowd* stepped up to self-govern, fix and solve issues, *together*. Indeed, *collaboration* is now coming to the fore. The *Gig Economy* may well be transitional and is currently largely transactional.

Yet, as it develops, research is pointing towards *collaboration* as a means of developing sustained business relationships.

For example, the formation of *work groups* enable *gig teams* to tackle a series of problems rather than a solitary issue.

If the *Gig Economy* is evolving towards sustained work groups, organisations need to evolve with it as we enter a more collaborative *Gig Economy*.

Meanwhile, I could see all around me that off shoring, on-shoring, outsourcing, agency contractors, permanent drives, *Preferred Supplier Lists (PSLs)* and *Recruitment Process Outsourcers (RPOs)* were just not cutting it at scale, or for emergent change.

I realised that we were on the tipping point of enterprise wanting to try something new.

And, whilst I knew this was unlikely to happen overnight, the stats around the rising failure of change programmes and even higher failure of digital transformation programmes, demonstrated that past practices were no longer going to help companies succeed.

According to *McKinsey*, *'70 per cent of change programmes fail to achieve their goals, largely due to employee resistance and lack of management support.'*

Yet change has become a necessity.

I wondered how we could lean into this change, rather than tie ourselves up in knots and use past practices that were fine getting people to 2017 but would not get them to 2027?

The 21st century is not going to wait for big monolithic organisations to try and change every multi-year period. It became apparent that the pace of change in innovation would just continue to pick up and challenge all models, keeping everyone perpetually on our toes.

That's a difficult place to succeed from.

Unless we could respond in such an agile way that we could stay ahead and enable our clients and candidates to do the same.

If only we could develop a model that would enable companies to align properly, plan sufficiently and partner well for the new flexible collaborative economy, so they'd be able to deliver on their critical initiatives while boosting business performance and internal capability.

I thought about what had made my own career such a success.

It feels odd to blow my own trumpet, but my clients often told me I was the best in the trade. So, whilst I blushed at the praise, it was important for me to figure out why I'd been voted as *Global Interim Recruiter of the Year 2015* by a major industry body, my peers, candidates and clients.

Why was I the right person to pioneer a new model that could influence profound change and spark a revolution?

During the last 15 years in business, I'd recruited IT leaders and senior contractors and Interim managers for many organisations across many industries and placed over 1000+ senior IT Interims into many successful IT programmes.

Prior to winning the *Global Interim* award, I had been the top salesman out of 600 recruiters world-wide and had co-built the largest independent technology and change recruitment company in the UK.

Given that I'd populated hundreds of transformations, I felt like I'd got a knack for creating and deploying successful high-performing teams who deliver.

I had been sketching out a way to turn the frustrations I'd uncovered into trust, by delving deeper into track records, tapping into referrals, gathering proof of results, and essentially, focusing on the personalised service of getting to know people.

I already knew from my own experience that nailing these three things – *people, processes* and *partners* - would generate a great result.

It was just a case of turning the *why* into the *how*.

Phase 3
Turning Frustration Into Opportunity -
My Vision For an Interim Revolution
which Harnesses The Power of The Crowd

My vision began to formulate. This vision, my *big game* is to spark and ignite an *Interim Revolution* to help organisations bolster their change capability – a revolution of talent and a genuine alternative to consulting firms.

But how? By harnessing the globe's intelligence and experience to build thriving communities and teams of Interim change agents and leaders all over the world, to solve business problems together. And, in doing so, create one of the first virtual global change partner crowd companies, powered by the Interim crowd.

Revolutions transform. They replace the status quo with a new world; a new way of operating. I could feel it in my bones that we were on the cusp of this Interim revolution and corporate transformation.

Interims can help prevent fast-growth corporates from becoming hierarchical by enabling them to decentralise and self-organise. By bringing together top 5% Interims which, as a group, create a revolution, we could empower and enable organisations to change how they operate, so they don't lose their edge.

By providing high performing people to crowd around a purpose to achieve business objectives and solve business problems, we can empower the more traditional established organisation to become more responsive and agile, like the new breed of organisations.

By providing the best independent expertise on tap and advisory on demand to deliver projects and provide auxiliary leadership whenever and however it's needed, we can make a positive impact, whilst also benefiting those executives currently working within the organisation. This is possible because these *guns for hire* have the capability and devotion to coach and guide your transformation with you.

This is how you're going to develop your best staff.

Your best staff want to do your best projects, not see you outsource again. They want to get involved in your best action. They don't want to do the mundane administrative operational work.

Some of that is going to get destroyed replaced by *Artificial Intelligence (AI)* and robotic process automation anyway.

People want to get real experience and real experience comes from changing organisations, hacking models, delivering projects, knowledge work and making an impact.

I truly believe that hiring Interims is the best way to do that.

It's not to come in and be your workforce, it's to help guide transformation, develop talent and be your voice of reason, to be your secret weapon in the background; the unsung heroes of the business world. Superheroes who can swoop in and close that capability gap and speed gap once and for all, whilst always looking to create and add value to you and the organisation.

And I could see that recruiters in the US were already transforming themselves into proper *on-demand agents,* rather than the commodity they are in the UK.

This fueled my core belief, that there is an incredible power at the intersection of a good recruiter and the Interim community.

But there was more to it than the provision of Interims.

If I was going to create a fresh model that enabled recruiters to embed themselves into the board's business plan and build more value around their own processes and those of their clients, I needed to find a model that had the potential to make a hugely positive impact to the clients' businesses as well as to the individual Interim, given the changing nature of work.

In the case of my own business, *Sullivan & Stanley*, I found *discovering and uncovering problems, trend-spotting* and *converting frustration into opportunity* - as an ongoing process - is useful in rethinking and refreshing my client offering.

The Power of The Collective:
Teams and The Hollywood Model

When I started to thoroughly explore what was happening in the States I subsequently had a major light bulb moment.

I realised that the C-Suite and recruitment world was all going in the direction of teams.

I had personally been designing Interim teams for many years, but iteratively.

I suddenly saw with crystal clear clarity how tapping into the combined mind-power and cohesive skillset of teams would be the future and that the *Interim Revolution* would be the way to get us there – to pre-gel teams of top notch Interims to deliver beyond expectations; to move on this opportunity to put the *law of teams* in the *Agile Manifesto* into practice.

As I researched further, I found that my solution to reducing the *capability* and *speed* gaps would be to recruit, cast and assemble flexible teams to tackle business problems.

It is no coincidence I was in Hollywood!

And that this is exactly the same way that Hollywood production companies assemble a team, make the movie and then disperse to the next project.

American recruiters are already doing this for rare developers, yet no one is doing it for change agents/stars. And every company needs a good change agent and structured teams of change agents to deal with emergent change as a guide.

Smaller and fully empowered teams are essential to help organisations with their agility, accelerated delivery and velocity.

Indeed, when we look at industries that have successfully evolved, they have done so because they are agile; they crowd around a project, deliver and move on.

There is so much talent to draw upon, they cast teams of the best people, just as Hollywood evolved from the death of the Big Studios, I see enterprises today evolving too.

By tapping into teams, corporations of all sizes can plug the purest form of agility into their operations without the time-consuming bloated processes involved in traditional recruitment processes for permanent staff.

The result is that businesses stay lean.

The future recruiter becomes the casting director, assembles teams from a curated network to deliver projects and keep the business in a continual state of transformation, whilst benefiting the organisation with credit as opposed to debt.

By bringing in teams at your leisure (sourced from the best network of well-built relationships) you, as an organisation, can flex the knowledge you need, when you want it, how you want it.

That is the heartbeat of this model – *teams of Interim stars on-demand*. Lean and keen.

After running my initial ideas past my network and receiving an abundantly positive reaction, I realised I was onto something.

So, I decided to get out there and act on a frustration I experienced daily from candidates and clients. I took the plunge to try to fix the system that is broken yet tolerated; left relatively unchallenged, probably because, until now, there had been no real alternative.

I left the comfort of a secure role to launch forth into the entrepreneurial process and create this *new way*. One that would enable clients to future proof their organisations.

This was something I had to embark on.

In early 2016, I set up *Sullivan & Stanley* – a challenger brand for an emergent world, a collective of top 5% change agents, leaders and recruiters who help our clients cope with the complexity of new world disruption, while doing a little disrupting ourselves.

I formed a group entitled *Executive Gigs* so that I could keep the conversation going.

I had considered calling the business *Lynes Associates*, but it didn't have the same ring to it and I wanted something that really inspired me on a daily basis; a name that was about the next generation.

Sullivan is my eldest son and Stanley is my youngest son. So each morning when I get up, seeing the name of my two sons – the next generation - above the door, inspires me greatly.

Something else that inspires me is this quote by American architect, systems theorist and inventor, Buckminster Fuller:

"You never change things by fighting the existing reality.
To change something, build a new model
that makes the existing model obsolete."

Building such a model is the conduit for me; between getting frustrated about the current state of the market and hearing all the collective sighs and groans and then doing something about it.

As well as building this model and getting it out into the marketplace, I wanted to write a book to explain the model, define why it is necessary and encourage leaders and business-es to take first principle thinking.

First Principles Thinking is a way of thinking that the likes of Elon Musk have popularised.

So, rather than doing something a way that it has always been done, we consider the situation as it is and then use our own considerations and reasoning to consider (or buy-into) solutions without defaulting to the traditional way of thinking about it. This involves taking risks and building up a tolerance for doing so because, let's face it, we all know of companies who have faltered or closed because of their risk-aversion in the face of sudden change.

This way of strategising also involves thinking long-term to consider where the business and industry is headed and likely to be in seven or more years time. Short-term thinking has created this problem, long-term thinking is what will solve it.

First Principles Thinking also has a lot to do with being obsessed with customer service and providing service that delights customers and exceeds expectations. The customer should take centre stage so, for recruiters, delivering the right people into their clients' organisations is the top priority, every single time.

Notably, all clients want is to be surrounded with great people; a trusted advisor *hired as a gun* to help their sponsor and organisation cope with 21st century change.

There isn't one client I've ever worked with who doesn't get excited when they hire a top 5% individual from me who genuinely makes a difference to their business, makes their life easier, is loyal to them and helps them drive simplicity out of complexity.

I put what I've achieved down to two core focuses:

- *Service-oriented community building*
- *Customer obsession*

The model I have created taps wonderfully into both of these two core focuses.

It puts the customer, relationships and networks at the forefront. And it optimises this on-demand, *Gig Economy* and proliferation of powerful people into the Interim market. It does so by tapping into the best talent to enable the provision of aligned teams from trusted hybrid recruitment and consulting partners.

For the first time in a long time – it enables the alignment of processes, people and partners.

By fusing the best of both worlds, (a hybrid of Interim recruitment and consultancy) the model I am about to show you offers a new composite approach, which enables organisations to draw upon the Interim resource, their know-how and capability, as and when they choose. To create flexible solutions that actually work, deliver and give you a sustainable capability.

Because successful transformation needs a different approach and different people, especially in a world where the whole concept of work has shifted.

Key Takeaways

- Disruptive change is here and inevitable. Boards need to lean into it and embrace the opportunities it creates.
- Technology innovation is driving rapid disruptive change and highlighting capability and speed gaps. You need to acknowledge and embrace this.
- Larger organisations are typically less agile and much slower to respond.
- The old model is placing individual Interims managed by you with the associated interview burden/debt.
- The new model is designing teams of pre-gelled, top-5%, *A-Team*, *Teams as a Service* Interims. The right people, the right expertise, at the right time.
- The new model is best illustrated by the Hollywood movie approach of assembling top 5%, *A-Teams* to work on projects that disperse once the project concludes.

Rapid Action points

- Reflect on your current change strategy and capability.
- How much do you rely on consulting partners?
- Is that working?

Chapter 2

The Future of Work

Chapter 2
The Future of Work: Lean, Agile, Freelance And Team-Based

The New World of Work

It is not just the level of expectation and the behaviour of business that has changed.

The behaviour of business, technological advances and the level of expectation have all shifted. But they are the norm and part of the changes impacting the world of business.

Work has changed too.

In the past, jobs were for life or, certainly more permanent, and you had to make the most of the skills you had or hire a whole new permanent person/team to deal with new challenges.

Today, aligned Interim teams of high-calibre talent work on single projects. Then they move on to the next project.

In the past, *profit* was the only measure of how good a company was.

Today, *purpose* is the critical measurement tool. Mission matters. As such, generational differences require more flexibility and, with *Millennials* now proliferating the workforce, companies need to be as purposeful as they are profitable, in order to attract and retain talent.

In the past, the corporate world was *closed* and *controlled* and the career ladder was steep to climb.

Today, the rise of the *Gig Economy* enables *collaboration* and *innovation* and taps into the new connected world of tight productive relationships. Interim managers fill the gaps at a high level and networks provide reassurance in an uncertain world. The best people perform at their best in each gig, building relationships, knowledge, influence and their respective networks.

In the past, candidates applied for jobs by sending their CV in to agencies and responding to ads.

Today, the best candidates (certainly our best associates) do not apply for adverts. They do not like their CV on a database, because they find it too frustrating to be just another number in a large agency machine and have generally lost confidence in the black hole of applying through *JobServe* via recruiters.

Many have stated they even doubt the integrity of the position.

The way people fundamentally find work and do work is already changing, and continues to do so. Not surprising, given there were no social networks over a decade ago. And if you work in the online marketing, web programming or mobile phone industries, your job didn't even exist 20 years ago.

Indeed, work is no longer a place that you go, it's a thing that you do, from anywhere. Job and location are now uncoupled. Location is therefore irrelevant, while relationships and communication are increasingly important.

According to *ODesk*, in this flat, transparent, accessible, innovative, crowdsourced world of work:

"The word 'career' is as outdated as the word 'typewriter.'"

That Was Then, This Is Now:
Shift Happens as The Old and New World Collide

"Why join the navy when you can be a pirate?"
Steve Jobs, Apple Founder

To cope with today's rate of change, companies need specialist knowledge and skills from people with a diverse range of experience on a project-by-project basis.

But they need it *yesterday*. And it's not optional.

As a heads-up take a look at some of key trends.

Old Thinking	New Thinking	Next Thinking
Interims are our biggest *cost*	Interims are our biggest *asset*	Interims are valued partners
Top-down communication	Open communication	Honest communication
Hire for skill	Hire for attitude and skill	Hire for buy-in and partnership
Time based work schedule	Focused working schedule	Flexible and outcome based work
Work for the weekend	Do something you love on a gig basis	Run a portfolio of opportunities
Enrich shareholders	Enrich lives	Enrich own mind
Hierarchy	Decentralisation	Self-organisation

Old Thinking	New Thinking	Next Thinking
Interim seeking high day rate (transactional)	Interim seeking high decision value-creating role	Interim creating a meaningful portfolio of opportunities with the ultimate objective of life through the work
Growth in position - corporate ladder climbing	Flexibility in career and journey	Fulfillment in career and enjoying the journey
Job as livelihood	Job as status and engagement	Job as an opportunity for meaning
Co-worker as a competitor	Co-worker as a colleague	Co-worker as a collaborator
Individuals	Groups and teams	Pre-gelled collaborative networked teams

And, while companies discover they need to tap into this talent to keep up, let alone stay ahead, talented people have simultaneously discovered that creating a flexible, work/life balance is no-longer a pipe dream.

They can maximise and optimise their output, their income and their strengths, in exchange for autonomy and a more balanced working life.

Welcome to the *Gig Economy* – where companies contracting independent workers for short-term engagements is increasingly commonplace; an evolution of the trend away from a job for life towards multiple job-changes over a working life.

For the majority of my career the *Gig Economy* simply didn't exist.

Yet, over the last few years, through the success of *AirBNB, Uber* and recruitment market places such as *Hired.com* and *Upwork.com*, the terminology is becoming more widespread and moving up into the white collar market to include, what I call, the *Knowledge and Executive Gig Economy.*

The candidates I interview tell me that the *Gig Economy* gives them the freedom to choose flexibility and dictate their own terms. It's a win-win, for both industries and individuals.

The good news is *crowdsourcing* and hiring freelance or Interim individuals and teams not only addresses the core needs of the enterprise; it also addresses the needs of the worker.

Your company, now with easy access to specific strategic expertise, (which would be less affordable to maintain on staff) becomes more lean and agile, increases speed to market and improves innovation into projects. And it's fit-for-purpose.

This way of working enables your company to conserve expensive resources in terms of training, office space and benefits.

Furthermore, they can select the very best people for specific projects from a much wider talent pool than traditionally available in a given location.

Meanwhile, the Interim gains control over their work-life balance with the ability to work from anywhere during hours that fit their lives (around childcare or other commitments – e.g., from 9am-3pm and 8pm-10pm). Consequently, Interims enjoy a wider pool of quality projects from around the world from which to choose.

People are building portfolio careers out of the projects they partake (and excel) in; and as a result *non-executive directors* (NEDs) and other *C-Suite* executives and managers are embracing the Interim workforce.

Workers under the age of 35 are indicating a preference to work as freelancers on a project-by-project basis. Workers over the age of 35 are indicating that they want to take their IP, experience and value to the Interim market.

Sufficient research indicates that *Millennials* are adapting to contracting at a faster rate than we've seen from previous generations. And many recruitment experts, along with publications such as *Forbes*, predict that 40% of people will be self-employed by 2020.

A recent *Way We Work* survey (2015) of 9,000 knowledge workers by *Unify* revealed that 52% already work in virtual teams. Marketplaces connecting progressive companies and disruptors with freelance talent are rife.

Surrounding this nucleus of change is an enabling environment that further drives these shifts. The rise in cloud computing and usage of technologies, such as *Skype* and *Zoom*, along with an increase in products and services aimed at the self-employed, further enables virtual working.

This has resulted in a huge rise in on-demand freelance workers, project-based staff and Interim executives. And, along with an imbalance between the supply and demand for tech talent, has turned the corporate talent management model on it's head.

Subsequently, world of work is also changing rapidly. *'Fortune favours the brave'* says a Latin proverb and, in the new world of work, fortune favours top in-demand talent and the smart companies who value that talent sufficiently to hire them on-demand.

From Gig Economy to an Executive Gig Economy

Non-strategic workers, such as contract cleaners, have been outsourced for many years, so the concept is not new.

However, in the past few years there has been a significant rise in the number of highly skilled, strategic, thought-leaders, knowledge-workers and change-agents entering the Interim management and freelance consultancy world. This network of agile talent is accessible through the right trusted partners.

The benefits they can bring to a business can be extraordinary.

The rise of this *Executive Gig Economy* - a phrase that I have coined while exploring this shift over the past couple of years - has empowered workers to concentrate on journeys over jobs where the experience and freedom is more coveted than the security of a job or a career path.

The future knowledge worker is demanding *flexibility*.

The corporate enterprise structure that doesn't provide this will continue to lose further talent to more progressive newer organisations who adopt future of work practices.

Predictably, the talent drain from permanent to flexible working is increasing.

The changing needs of today's workers, the war for talent, rise of the *Gig Economy* (and Executive *Gig Economy*) and the future of work; all of these forces combined are driving workforce management to the top of the business agenda, especially as talent becomes one of the only true differentiators of success nowadays.

However, the *Gig Economy* doesn't have to be threatening.

There's a huge opportunity for businesses here, and a large pool of flexible, highly skilled workers to tap into on-demand. Enterprises and the *C-Suite* have a real opportunity to tap into a scalable workforce that can help them meet the business agendas needs, whilst also benefiting the core operation.

As the workload and delivery demands increase, you can access the right people with the right set of skills to come in and work with you.

The result is predictable high quality delivery and the ability to close the capability and speed gaps in an uncertain world.

Why would you rely on one individual member of staff when you can tap into the diverse range of expertise from a wide range of high quality sources? Many of whom would be prohibitively pricey if you were to hire them as full-time permanent staff or from management consulting firms.

Access to premium diverse skills and expertise has never been so prevalent. In essence, the *Gig Economy* is connecting those with high-end knowledge and capability to organisations in dire need of those skills, which ordinarily just wouldn't have access to them.

And, whilst smaller agile firms are benefiting hugely by bringing freelancers and part-time Interims in to their workforce, larger companies are too and more so.

For example, one of the biggest management consulting firms, *PWC,* launched a *Talent Exchange* platform in the US and is growing its freelance and Interim workforce exponentially.

Consequentially, the *Gig Economy* is significantly impacting the future of work across businesses *of all sizes.*

However, in order for corporates to optimise the positive effect of tapping into this talent, they need reassurance about the quality of hires in this new landscape.

Indeed, research by the *Recruitment and Employment Federation* (REC) revealed that 20% of businesses see that the risks of incorporating digital work platforms into their hiring strategies outweigh the benefits, with a key concern being the certainty of access to high-quality talent.

This means that recruitment strategies and processes must be aligned with the prime people required.

The best way to achieve this is to hire a *trusted partner* with a high-quality network who can source the best available talent and skills base. As a result, that partner will be able to secure individuals and teams who fit with precise needs.

Ultimately, freelance/Interim work is not just an emerging trend. It's the new normal, the new way of working.

So, the sooner organisations embrace this way of working, (as an enabler, rather than a cost) the more empowered they will be in the future, as the competition for high quality tech and strategic executive talent becomes even fiercer.

A recent *Deloitte* report, *The Open Talent Economy* explains:

> *"The evolving workforce is a mixture of employees, contractors and freelancers, and - increasingly - people with no formal ties to your enterprise at all.*
>
> *The consultancy defines open talent as 'a collaborative, transparent, technology-enabled, rapid-cycle way of doing business. What the open source model did for software, the open talent economy is doing for work', the report says, concluding, 'In this new economy, access to talent is more important than ownership of talent.'"*

Talent access is the elixir that the *Gig Economy* offers tired enterprises who face constant talent uncertainty today.

Unfortunately, the cost of the upheaval of perm attrition, non-stop recruiting, the interview overheads on your management layer and on-boarding is more than just monetary. The instability can have a pronounced negative effect on overall productivity and an enterprise's ability to execute and innovate. The knock on effect of focusing on talent ownership over talent access can therefore be potentially devastating. Conversely, focusing on a trusted partnership strategy that enables enterprises to make the most of access to quality talent networks can be potentially revolutionary.

I've seen programmes abandoned with millions of pounds grossly wasted because of IT and change capacity limitations.

I've seen projects/programmes with big slippage in completed dates due to lack of access to key talent or by choosing the wrong partner and making poor front end decisions. And it is my own frustration around this and the frustration of the hundreds of CIOs I have interviewed, that has led to my writing this book.

Evidently, given the pace of change, companies will have to continually reinvent themselves.

So it's time to embrace change and ensure there is sufficient change capability to tap into, not only to win this war on talent, but as a business imperative.

Particularly within the IT space.

With change comes enablers - technology being one of them. It enables businesses to do more and faster. However, in order to maximise its enabling capacity, you need IT talent to plan, develop, test and support it. Notably, competition is fierce for these critical hires, which has created this war on talent in the first place.

Few are immune from this ongoing battle, which results in a never-ending bid to find and retain good people.

The problem is that a large percentage (around 25%, according to *Appirio.com*) of IT talent leaves the organisation which hired it each year. Not surprising, given that the best of the bunch are headhunted so frequently (recruiters approach top end IT talent as often as five times per day).

So, even if you spend well and motivate sufficiently, chances are you'll still lose your prized IT hires (your top technology/change talent with the right attitude and mindset) as the competition hots up.

The cost of this regular upheaval is high, as continuous recruiting and onboarding impacts productivity levels. I've seen first hand so many projects abandoned or fail to deliver desired outcomes and this has a knock on effect of repelling the talent required to sufficiently turn the tide in your favour.

So, what is a CIO/CTO to do when even well-paid, engaged, full time technology staff are in danger of being poached by smaller purpose-led agile start ups and with talent drain into the *Gig Economy*?

The solution is to shift towards crowdsourcing project-based work over full time employees; to hire teams and agile networks specifically brought in to crowd around specific problems; and deliver desired outcomes, whilst upskilling your core perm team, rather than outsource and lose both control and IP.

Outsourcing, offshoring and onshoring for knowledge work has failed to reduce the talent gap or win the war on talent, so crowdsourcing within the *Gig Economy* has become a fresher alternative.

Because, what has outsourcing really done for companies?

It has eroded trust and cost them millions, and it hasn't developed them a sustainable capability. Often times it has given the good quality permanent people cause to leave.

Conversely, with crowdsourcing, you can leverage the *Gig Economy* to source solutions from the best minds in the world within a flexible talent pool. This helps you plough through projects and solve problems at a much faster rate.

Of course, how companies hire is just one part of the solution. How companies organise their operations is also key.

Centralised vs Decentralised

There is a duality in the shifts we are seeing.

On the one hand we have the move towards agile talent and the on-demand-per-project workforce.

On the other there exists an opportunity to move away from a centralised organisational structure towards a decentralised structure. Both strands of change feed each other's evolution.

Currently, centralised structures rely on a few executives making key decisions and providing direction for the company.

Small businesses often use this structure, since the owner is responsible for the company's business operations. This can be an efficient way to run a business as entrepreneurs typically develop the company's mission and vision, and set objectives for managers and employees to follow when achieving these goals.

Decentralised organisational structures feature teams of individuals responsible for making business decisions and running the business close to the customer.

Reliance is placed more heavily on a team environment at different levels in the business. Individuals at each level in the business may have some autonomy to make business decisions.

This results in a more *open, agile, inclusive* and *collaborative* culture which utilises individuals with a variety of expertise and knowledge for running various business operations.

A broad-based diverse management team such as this helps ensure the company has knowledgeable directors or managers to handle various types of business situations and deal more readily with change.

My core belief is that organisations need to flex into a more decentralised way of operating and working, so that decisions are made as close as possible to where the work actually happens. You only have to look at the success of businesses like *Netflix* and *Zappos* to recognise this is a viable way to operate. I believe Interim leaders and change agents have a big role to play in this impending transformation.

Indeed, based on the increasing corporate need for high-quality specialists with a diverse range of skills, building communities of such talent and providing value to those communities is surely the future for recruiters.

The alternative is a continual *race-to-the-bottom* for commodisation of lower-quality talent; or high-cost, out-of-touch management consulting firms.

Driving Forces, and Emerging Trends
– The Sharing Networked Economy

Along with the rise of the *Gig Economy*, we are now living in a *network economy* or *sharing economy* which has made the world smaller and talent and strategic alliances more readily accessible. This is good news.

Secondly, another driving force of change is the generational differences of those entering the workforce.

Millennials and *Generation Y* want to work *with* companies rather than *for* them and it is this purpose-driven work ethic that has created a requirement for companies to up their game and prioritise value-adding, meaningful missions to attract the high-quality, younger talent coming through.

Ultimately, this is where the world is going.

If you don't have purpose, you aren't going to be fit for purpose. It's as simple as that. Just as, if you don't have plans in place to deal with digital disruption and get on board with technological transformation, you are going to struggle in this digital age.

Such driving forces and emerging trends are creating a world where a new way of working with and hiring people has been firmly established. Along with the rise of the *Gig Economy*,

it's transforming the nature of the workforce forever.

The Network Economy: Project Team Power

In the past, if you wanted to partner with or connect with others you needed to get past gatekeepers to arrange a face-to-face meeting.

Today, each individual is connected across a global network of communities and that connectivity is accelerating exponentially. We each link in to other networks creating a seamless labyrinth, where we are each only a few introductions away from all the people we could hope to connect with.

This creates network upon network, making the top talent accessible, actually tangibly hire-able, right now. You can now source the absolute *crème de la crème* to work with you on your projects.

You can tap into the top talent to help you through the unrelenting uncertainty and continual change.

You can also find trusted and capable partners to bring those individuals and teams to you.

Certainly, as the pace of connection accelerates, if you connect with the right people, you can harness the power of the trusted network to propel your business forward, onward and upward in the midst of continual change.

These networks, alongside the rise of the *Gig Economy* have created a culture of community, a sharing economy, where people crowd around a project in networks of teams to deliver specific outcomes.

Consequently, the future is all about *networks* and *teams*.

Hollywood As The Heartbeat

Although becoming more ubiquitous, the network economy is nothing new. There is a lot of rhetoric in the States about the network economy and some fascinating analogies around the construction and movie industries. Both have been part of network economies for some time and are reaping the rewards. In the construction sector, for instance, contractors, subcontractors, and skilled employees all come together for an outcome – to create or re-develop a building or housing project. This diverse range of professionals come together specifically for an outcome and then disperse onto another outcome, leaving the core business to flex up and down upon demand and changing market conditions.

And consider the Hollywood model. Hollywood Studios used to employ tens of thousands of people to make films – now they *crowdsource* them around a film.

Hence why many change agents are drawing inspiration from the transformation that the movie industry has been through, with Hollywood as the heartbeat.

I particularly like this prime example of the network economy, because of the transformation it's been through over the last 50 years; from an industrially organised sector into a network economy, during which new opportunities, markets and challenger firms emerged and replaced the departments in the old industrial hierarchies.

The industry is thriving today and both the independent movie companies and the interwoven network of teams, which work together to create the final products, are benefiting from this temporary team-based re-organisation.

Learning lessons from the decentralised Hollywood model may seem off piste, but the movie industry actually offers the closest example in existence right now of what the future of work will likely be for the rest of us.

But it clearly demonstrates why recruiters need to have a paradigm shift from recruiting individuals iteratively to recruiting temporary teams for business benefit. Because the recruitment model as we know it is dying.

Focused, purposeful people generate better business outcomes.

The Hollywood network of teams model has been proving why it's good to have self-organising virtual teams of people crowding round missions and problems, and they've been proving this for some time.

Their team members have a purpose, they have a focus and they produce much better outcomes than hierarchies and rules and process and governance. Not only that, what might ordinarily be a lonely existence as a sole trader, teaming up with others bolsters their creativity and capability.

Clearly, they are stronger *together*.

This is why I believe that decentralisation, which mirrors the Hollywood modus operandi, can enable business organisations today. Especially ones stuck with organisational and technical debt. Teams can solve problems, whilst freeing up executives to concentrate on the innovation agenda – a win-win.

One view, which I heartily agree with, is that larger organisations will need to decentralise into manageable chunks in order to deliver real change and close the capability gap. Networks will be created around specific projects, then switch to other networks as soon as a project is completed.

This enables organisations to stay lean, pivot around rapid changing market variables and concentrate on value creation and innovation at their core. In doing so, they put the customer back into the heart of the organisation.

However, there are some vital considerations to bear in mind when looking to move from a centralised operation to a decentralised one, because it's critical to ensure that the 'as is', - what's working for the business currently - still operates well.

With our model, we take this consideration and then set up a kind of parallel universe where the new operating model sits.

During the first six to nine months, a team will help the client cross the chasm to this parallel new operation model.

This gives the organisation three speeds of delivery for the business; to respect the current revenue model, whilst creating the future revenue(s) model:

- The original operating model, which is generating revenues and contains people who are happy to continue operating there.
- The gradual shift.
- The accelerated delivery into the new state of the organisation. Bespoke teams models, such as ours, will enable this transition and ensure that change is enabling rather than crippling.

I believe that this whole approach is how traditional bureaucracy-laden *FTSE* and *Fortune* corporations, which struggle to change amid their prevalent revenue vs innovation dilemma, will find a way to overcome this struggle towards a more responsive and agile future.

I strongly believe that it is great teams who will carry enterprises onward just as it is great teams who unite in Hollywood to create box-office blockbusters before moving on to the next project.

And this is a new status quo that, following the demise of large corporates, actually works. Notably, when the Hollywood studio system crumbled, amazing movies did not.

Teams are effective and powerful in the modern age as Hollywood and other industries demonstrate.

Teams Enable Agility

Another benefit of teams is the empowered focus they create and perpetuate. Small teams create a start-up mentality, which equips companies with a creative ability to think of ways to become and stay lean.

Take music company, *Pandora's* prioritisation process, for example. Despite the Internet radio, music streaming and recommendation engine's huge valuation, and half a billion in revenues, having to pay much of its revenue to the rights holders within the music industry caused a creative, lean-thinking start-up mentality.

This led to *Pandora* chiefs inviting focused ideas from its wider team around the precise features that could be built quickly for maximum growth; i.e., the work that would matter most and be most valuable at any given time.

Rather than fail fast and try lots of things, they focused on *what they'd be foolish not to do* over the following 90-day period.

Large numbers of ideas would flow in but the management team decided on a cost per engineer and would gage how long each project might take and whether each of the ideas (pitched on just one slide) had the required features to sustain competitive advantage.

In order to maintain this nimble focus, rather than have the entire team of 40 engineers deciding which features to work on, the prioritisation team was tiny and made up of between three and five of the executive staff only.

Between them they would collaboratively figure out which 20 or so out of 400 ideas would make the shortlist.

This process was inclusive enough to motivate the wider team, but focused enough to make prioritisation part of the culture of *Pandora*.

Even after the IPO, *Pandora* divided its staff into small teams, all of which managed their own prioritisation process and backlog. And, despite growing from 40 engineers to 80 engineers, small teams were still empowered to make their own decisions, because *Pandora* had always understood the power of small teams and ensured that each team was furnished with the expertise to do so.

In this way, *Pandora* was able to achieve so much from a *less is more* approach.

Small autonomous teams operating in a decentralised way are more agile and lean and can enable improved focus, as long as the expertise exists within each, which is where the Interim model comes in.

Power To The People:
Harnessing The Power of The Collective

Although we can't predict what will happen in the future any more, we can say unequivocally that it will be the people who work for you who will make the difference between whether your company flies or falters.

It will also be the manner in which you hire those people that will either deliver or diminish value in those models of recruitment and in your company going forward. For the world of recruitment and consulting has been equally affected by change as other industries. We're all in this together.

Yet one constant remains; the fact that people are a company's biggest asset.

That fact holds true and is unchanging. How those people work and deliver may have shifted, but, if you ask any CEO of any company, regardless of size, they will all agree that hiring and retaining people is their biggest challenge. Why? Because people matter so much.

- People make a difference
- Good people can be hard to find and keep
- Great people are rare
- Great teams are even rarer

Ultimately, it is only through collective brains uniting together that we can solve today's problems and figure out better ways of doing business in an ever-changing world.

Which is where this book comes in.

Key Takeaways

- There is a serious talent drain from permanent to flexible working i.e., the knowledge *Gig Economy* is increasing.
- The future worker is demanding flexibility, variety and focused gig work. The corporate enterprise structure that doesn't provide this will continue to lose further talent to more progressive organisations.
- The *Executive Gig Economy* gives you on-demand access to specific strategic expertise that is flexible and incredibly cost-effective.
- The game has changed from ownership of talent to access to talent.
- The future of work is a win-win for both the enterprise and the individual.
- Hollywood and the construction industry offer a prime example of the network economy - focused teams crowding around a project to deliver results.

Rapid Action Points

- Reflect on the way you view Interims. Do you see them as a cost or valued assets? Do you use Interims to coach and upskill your permanent staff?
- Start to rethink the way your business can respond to changes in the market. Try an experiment and assemble a small team around a mission and/or outcome. Nimble, fast-moving teams can stay one step ahead of the consumer, completing work faster and more efficiently.
- Give these teams special sponsorship to cut through the bureaucracy. Analyse the speed, efficiency and effectiveness compared to a delivery team inside the business and current processes.
- The future is Agile, mission based teams. Are you ready to attract and retain the next generation of *Gig* talent?

Chapter 3

The Recruitment and Consulting Trap
And What It Costs You

Chapter 3
The Recruitment and Consulting Trap
And What It Costs You

*"The best asset the world has is not oil or money but people
and collective brains of the world to solve today's problems."*
Paul Frampton, CEO of Havas UK

People As A Commodity

Consider companies that are doing really well.

Typically they put recruitment to the top of their priority list and they don't outsource their strategy. They know that the only real differentiator is the human assets you've got in your business and the collection of minds those people offer you.

That's a given in a secure and certain world.

OK, so we agree: people matter.

But when change is constant, talent is draining towards the *Gig Economy* and change management programmes are failing; the need to put positive recruitment first and prioritise that collection of minds becomes all the more pressing. Notably, in this environment, the right people matter a whole lot more. It is people who make the difference in business, even more so when the landscape is uncertain.

And yet, having been in the recruitment industry for 15 years, I've noticed the increasing commoditisation of the provision of people, which is creating a bad value exchange for all parties. And it's not just the bloated inflexible corporations being left behind, but all those who enter the recruitment trap; a trap shaped by a myriad of industry and client-side mistakes.

The reality is that, within the past decade, I've seen hundreds of organisations struggling to consistently find the help they need to recruit Interim leaders and senior IT contractors.

The consensus is that IT and change recruitment is a nightmare; a *dark art* littered with so many variables internally and externally that are difficult to mitigate against, creating many problems.

The current backdrop has created an eco-system with little trust, minimal value with a morass of partners all offering similar services with no real differentiator. Couple this with the growing talent drain into the *Gig Economy*, the skills gap - which is widening daily - and the sheer pace of 21st-century change, many organisations are now left woefully exposed and unprepared for the future.

Basically, companies are losing their best people and hiring their worst. And recruiters are letting down the companies who trust them.

Change agents especially are seeking to avoid the large bloated organisations where delivery is a frustrating pipe dream; where bureaucracy and waste are the business currency. Unfortunately for the larger enterprise, this is the prevalent view from my network.

Of course, day-rate contractors and industrial mindset permanent staff are still easy to source. But without the right trusted partners and processes in place to secure any top 5% talent or candidates with an emergent change mindset, you are going to struggle to attract that type of person.

Yet they are exactly the type of people that you need.

Thankfully, mistakes can be the catalyst towards success. I've made plenty, but I've learned from them. Mistakes are great learning tools.

However, in this crazy-paced corporate environment where the only certainty is change itself, problems can spiral out of control and compounded mistakes can exaggerate problems that need solving. Far better then to learn from mistakes outlined in the pages that follow.

Because *not* taking action is costly.

Especially when the talent drain into the *Gig Economy* and Interim/contract workforce is rising. Especially when so many companies, due to broken recruitment and consulting processes and the pressure to place people, are hiring under duress and settling for second best.

Frankly, when you compound that problem, with over 100 people in a change programme, there is only one result: *failure*.

The Cost Of Compounded Problems = Organisational Debt

To be clear:

- *Organisational Credit* is the interest companies accrue when their structures and policies are flexible and decentralised to flex as the world changes
- *Organisation Debt* is the interest companies pay when their structure and policies stay fixed and/or accumulate as the world changes

Of course, when something like the world of work shifts so exponentially whilst the mechanisms that fuel it stay the same, problems are always going to arise.

So, when the practice of hiring people doesn't change to reflect the shift in work practices, the impact is always going to be hard-hitting.

And when the impact trickles down throughout the entire organisation as mistakes are compounded, the result can generate catastrophic *organisational debt* that is difficult to recover from.

Here's what I have noticed.

Within recruitment and consulting – the models for leaders and knowledge workers, each of the various available options are currently failing.

- The iterative recruitment agency option is a lottery and puts the organisation under too much interview and management burden.
- The consultancy option is expensive and flawed, often keeping you in the problem. Years of outsourcing has already demonstrated that it doesn't leave you with a capability.
- Procurement, HR, CFO decisions to bring in a *one-size-fits-all* master agreement (i.e., Recruitment Process Outsourcer) model, which is more of a *one-size-doesn't-fit-at-all* model.

Recruitment agencies, *Recruitment Process Outsource* companies, *Preferred Supplier Lists* and *body-shoppers*, through their lack of personalisation and lack of investment in clients or candidates, have created a low-value recruitment lottery. This causes companies to ask, *why not just do this ourselves?*

This has created a broken value exchange where there is a worrying lack of science in the critical decision making process of hiring good people.

Consequently, the talent provided is often low-calibre and trust in the recruitment industry is faltering. This is encouraging organisations to cut out the intermediary, i.e., the recruitment agency, the very establishments that were set up to serve them.

After all, in a changing world where the future is uncertain and less is predictable, the last thing any company needs is a recruitment lottery.

Rather, organisations today need recruitment certainty, along with partners and people they can trust to deliver on point and fast, to keep up with the increasing pace of change and pace of connection.

The continual state of change merely heightens the problem as companies aren't ready for transformation and aren't sure what problems they are trying to solve.

Subsequently, planning and alignment falls by the wayside as enterprises are unsure what a great person really looks like and, in some cases, don't have the clarity on exactly what they're looking for.

Finding a trusted partner for IT and business change becomes increasingly difficult as companies struggle to source anyone who can help them solve these emerging business problems.

This leads to client-recruiter frustration and nobody wins.

Yet, without a clear solution, it's difficult to know who to trust.

Broken Value Exchange vs Value Networks: The Happy Value Chain

Over the past 15 years I've helped many organisations change, integrate, rationalize and deliver key programmes of work through recruiting and mobilising small and large teams of Interims.

The key ingredient to this success has been a true partnership with the client. One where I'm working alongside them, understanding the ideal world outcomes they desire and result paths to delivering whatever the career and Interim assignment is dependent on.

The golden rule I've always lived by is that *a client should be for life.*

It's crucial to take time to understand cultural fit, alignment to client and alignment to the environment.

So, I've dedicated my career to finding and sourcing the best contract consultants and Interim leaders, through incessant networking, referrals from the best and treating people like you would treat your family and friends. In my world, that has always led to an abundance of recommendations from the passive candidates, who don't like the agency circuit and rarely need to sell themselves, alongside strong recommendations to potential clients.

This way of working has served me and the clients I serve well.

The end result is a happy value chain where trust is pervasive and opportunities are in abundance.

Clients understand the true value of the recruitment industry.

Like Hollywood, good agents are worth their weight in gold. This insight has driven my career ever since.

Back then, I would spend half a day on site, speaking to stakeholders and interviewing team members. Aspirations and outcomes were discussed in detail and three culturally aligned personality matched Interims were sourced who were experts in the required area.

However, it feels that this type of personalised service is under threat right now in the UK knowledge worker contractor industry.

This happy value chain; the value network which enables parties to connect with each other, thereby creating value for all participants, is what needs to replace the current recruitment partnering system, i.e. the broken value exchange.

Frankly, I've never experienced as much frustration in the market about the current models that perpetuate our industry, as I have over the past few years.

This frustration is coming from clients, recruiters and candidates alike; from all three stakeholders.

This has led me to question: *where is this industry headed?*

So much so that I would sit in my office and frequently face-palm at the disarray unfolding before me.

"It's just such a struggle to find resilient, battle-hardened project staff, with empathy", a CIO would tell me. "There's no personal touch any more," another would add.

And so I watched as this industry faced struggle after struggle.

I didn't want to let that happen. I figured, the best way to do something about this sorry state of affairs was to speak to those affected by it – CIOs trying to recruit top IT talent to enable change and specialist IT contractors, change agents, delivery professionals and Interim leaders.

So I took the leap.

The subsequent feedback I gleaned from the insight of these 100 executives was astonishing, but not surprising.

As a result of digging deeper, I have uncovered the core problems at the heart of the industry.

Doing so gave me hope as I realised that a better way could be created to solve the problems that the majority of business leaders and CIOs are facing each day. I realised that through communicating this fresh framework, I could – through my own service provision of this unique model around teams, and through this book - continue to help good companies find good people and manage change effectively; to enable them not just to survive, but thrive.

However, before we can carve out a genuine solution that has the capacity to impact an entire industry, we need to dig deep amongst this huge pile of problems to understand why they exist? What is causing them? And what needs to happen in order to solve them?

The Real-Life Everyday Problems Faced and the 7 Mistakes Causing Them

Unfortunately, the majority of end user clients see recruitment agencies and consultancies as a necessary evil as there is a lack of viable alternatives available to them. It hasn't always been this way, but there are many reasons why it is now.

Fundamentally, there is a mismatch of objectives.

- The leaders and executives want good talent
- HR/Procurement/Finance want the cost benefit

The good recruitment agencies want to deal direct to line and engage with the business, but the lower margin commodity *race-to-the-bottom* doesn't encourage this. The client is left with poorly-skilled recruiters who don't vet and aren't adding value to the client.

This lack of planning (client-side) and lack of service (agency-side) isn't working. The candidates they are talking to are left with a distinct *cattle-market* feeling.

Consequently, the value exchange has become misaligned.

So, we have a broken exchange and total mess and something needs to be done.

During the interview sessions with these 100 executives, I uncovered and defined the core problems that they faced when hiring talent, including buying mistakes that caused buyer's remorse.

Some issues are caused by the client's mistakes. Others are caused by failures within the recruitment and consulting industry.

So, let's discover how not to recruit, by learning from these mistakes so we may avoid repeating them.

The Top 7 Avoidable Mistakes Made In Recruitment & Consultancy (and how *not* to recruit)

In a nutshell, the problems being experienced right now can be boiled down to three key issues.

- **Poor Planning/Alignment**
  You are not going to deliver real change, if you're not ready for transformation, if you don't know what you want and if you haven't aligned your processes, people and partners accordingly.

- **Poor Quality/Value**
  Where's the value in today's market? The lack of scientific vetting in the decision process for knowledge workers, the current recruitment fee structure and pressure to deliver low margin services results in poor quality service and poor quality talent. Outsourcing your recruitment or strategy, whether to an *RPO* or consulting firm, just isn't providing the value companies deserve or a sustainable change capability.

- **Poor Partnerships/Trust-Level**
  You have to surround yourself with great people – internally and externally – people you can trust. Doing so will reduce your time/cost and knowledge loss over the long-term and deliver *Organisational Credit*

rather than *Debit*. But who do you go to?
Recruitment agencies are a lottery, management consulting firms have eroded people's trust and going through your extended network is a big drag on your time. Plus, you're *not* a recruiter, you want a partner you can trust to give you great people and great solutions. But that's missing. So who can you turn to?

These are the issues that need highlighting, which I feel are totally avoidable.

Before we continue, for the benefit of those who are not involved in recruitment, here is a glossary of terms, which defines what those terms mean in a literal sense, but also, what those terms mean in a business and change management sense.

- **Preferred Supplier Lists (PSL)**
  A list of suppliers with uniform supply arrangements, payment terms and service levels. These are low margin mechanisms to save cost. However, they don't give you the best people. Poor agencies equal poor results.

- **Recruitment Process Outsourcing (RPO)**
  This is a type of *business process outsourcing* (BPO) where all or part of an employer's recruitment processes are transferred to an external service provider.
  My view is that you should never outsource your talent outcome for knowledge workers, it's too important. This is, fundamentally, a broken *one size fits all model* that will not be your segue to the next decade.
  The only way to get there is to prioritise your people.

- **Management Consulting Firms**
  Management consulting aims to help organisations improve performance, primarily through the analysis of existing problems and then developing plans for improvement. Historically, organisations that don't understand the problem tend to outsource the solution of

problems to management consulting firms which I believe is a false economy. You should be cautious about outsourcing your problem or solution strategy without retaining some ownership. Furthermore, it's important to consider who you partner with carefully, because, sometimes consultants want to keep you in the problem. Why? Because, as soon as the problem is solved, they can no longer invoice you.

So, let's explore these top seven mistakes in detail, so that you can avoid them and make people your priority in this new world of working.

The seven key mistakes are:

1. Reactive recruitment
2. Interview debt
3. Obsession with cost
4. Hiring a *Recruitment Process Outsourcer (RPO)*
5. Busting the *Preferred Supplier* myth
6. Entering the recruitment lottery in the first place
7. Falling into the expensive consultancy pyramid trap

Mistake 1. Reactive Recruitment

Poor planning creates a lack of alignment between the who, what, where, when, why and how of business i.e., the key dependencies that make a business successful:

- Who the people need to be in terms of skills, values, behaviour and personality/culture match
- What they need to be doing in terms of role
- Where the business is now and where it needs to get to
- Why and how so in terms of business/IT strategy and the processes and partners that will enable that

This misalignment leads to one common result: *hiring the wrong people.*

However, it's not just the lack of alignment that is at fault, but the lack of planning. In fact, it is the lack of planning which creates this flow of misalignment in the first place, which wastes time and loses business advantage.

Reactive recruitment as opposed to proactive recruitment is perhaps the biggest mistake of them all - because clients often don't know what they want or need.

They want good people and yet they don't know what good looks like. They haven't taken the time to pause and discover their needs, which creates a lack of clarity.

This is passed on to those involved in the recruitment process.

So no wonder the volume of mis-hires who don't fit what the business needs is rising.

Lack of clarity results in lack of correlation and wastes so much time. It is far wiser to invest time upfront at planning stage to get clear on the role, behaviours and fit required; but the majority of companies are finding this out the hard way. In fact, in many cases recruiters are three stages away from the real decision-maker. How are they expected to get to the core of what is needed talent-wise?

Fundamentally, too many people are involved in the recruitment decisions.

Lack of planning and a feeling that they were entering into the recruitment process without clarity around core needs came out as one of the top key problems that executives face today. You can't get clear on this without some discovery time. Yet, most interviewees revealed that agencies don't invest sufficient time at the start of the process to really drill the need out of the client, whilst clients often don't invest adequate time up front to think about what they want and consequently waste time interviewing with multiplicity.

Another observation was the failure of line managers to adequately define job roles, the culture and required behaviours so that role sizing and development takes place during interviewing rather than before. As such, interview time is often used by managers to crystalise their thoughts around what they want, wasting both company and candidates time.

Recruiting reactively rather than pro-actively; and failing to take the time to clarify the core requirements, led to problems with candidate flexibility and an inability to find the right mind-set for a particular mandate. Conversely, taking *discovery* time to understand the problem that needs solving and mapping out the exact skillset that will help solve that problem enables companies to get ahead of the curve.

And here is the first ironic part of the recruitment story – companies don't spend enough time up front planning but they spend way too much time interviewing.

Which leads us on to *Mistake #2.*

Mistake 2. Interview Debt: Companies Interview Far Too Many Candidates To Get The Talent

From my numerous interviews, one core problem came out on top: *hiring under duress as a result of broken, time-consuming processes and poor recruitment partners equals massive interview debt.* This is the unspoken problem of today's business world. No-one talks about how many interviews it takes to get talent.

Ultimately, decisions felt rushed because of the pressure to find someone fast, so companies frequently opted to take a punt after fatigue from too much interviewing. So much so that hiring under duress has become the status quo.

But why do so when so much is counting on securing the best assets you can find? The answer is time-sensitive.

People felt the recruitment process takes so long that they ended up settling for second best, because holding out for the best would prove too costly and time-consuming. We'll get onto the cost myth in due course.

But it's clear that broken processes are causing corporations (certainly those I interviewed) to miss out on talent.

Ultimately, the process is often so time-consuming and inefficient that companies often end up hiring sub-standard resource, which negatively impacts the wider project/programmes.

However, the problem doesn't end there, because the frustration created by mis-hiring, often leads to knee-jerk reactions about what to do next, which is often to spend out on consultancy.

This has it's own problems (see *Mistake #7*) and thus a perpetual loop of wrong-hires is created, time is wasted and business advantage is lost. So why does the process have to take so much time? What are the pain points here? Well, time-consuming over-interviewing seems to be a key issue.

Ironically, the lack of time spent clarifying the hard and soft skills, behaviours in various circumstances, values, durability and mindset of the ideal candidates, leads to more time spent during the interviewing process. Furthermore, those interviews take the business leaders' focus away from driving outcomes, so the time cost is doubled. As such, interviews are seen by many as *a blunt instrument*, failing to get into the core of the candidate.

I was told by a number of interviewees that, *too much time is wasted interviewing average candidates who've often over-sold themselves.*

This has to do with poor vetting and lack of science in the decision making process – another part of the broken process (see *Mistakes #3-#6*). Evidently, time spent up front planning and vetting is the most valuable part of the process.

The other reason that the recruitment process is taking too long is that too many people are involved in the process. This can make the route to talent torturous as HR get involved, alongside on-site leaders and procurement. Too many cooks spoil the broth indeed.

Consequently, those I spoke to felt they couldn't get talent quick enough due to the time it took searching for it, who often times, turned out not to be the right people after all (because of the lack of clarity, alignment and planning at the outset of the process). See what I mean about self-perpetuating loop?

Additionally, the red tape and bureaucracy of big company recruitment processes was flagged up as root cause of the lack of agility when it came to making vital recruitment decisions.

Such bureaucracy proves to be a restrictive headache for many.

On top of the process constraints of HR, procurement, and *PSL*, being too bloated and not agile enough has turned the recruitment headache into a migraine.

Mistake 3. Obsession With Cost

Business people worry about monetary cost and time cost because, in business, things often take longer and cost more than you initially think they will.

It's a given in business.

Because of this and the core business driver of profitability, business leaders become obsessed with anything that can save them time and money. But, when saving money is prioritised over the quality of people provision, problems begin to emerge.

However, spending less is a false economy.

We all know this as consumers - *you get what you pay for* in this world.

Cheap products do not last as long as those we spend more on. The same is true of services. I am noticing now more than ever that cheap front-end decisions are creating so many back-end problems.

Cheap does not beget value. To get a cheap price you always need to cut *quality* or *quantity - or both*.

Investing less when it comes to recruitment is not good value. Every little does *not* help.

Recruitment is not *Tesco*. It is a science of matchmaking and relationship-building and communication where quality costs more but pays in the long-term.

Unfortunately, many organisations, in a bid to save money, waste time. They do this by battling it out at the lower end of the food chain.

This *race to the bottom* that sacrifices quality for transition cost has created this bad value exchange.

Conversely, I have repeatedly found that three amazing people will create tangible savings and generate more profits, as opposed to spending on ten average people.

Focusing on the *cost* and not the *value* of that cost is one of the most detrimental mistakes that companies are making today.

Interviewees told me that their companies so frequently overspend on programme budgets but quibble on a few hundred pounds for one Interim who could save millions. Instead they opt for low-cost *body-shopping* or *Recruitment Process Outsourcing (RPOs)* which saves money in the short term but wastes more money than it saves in the long-term.

Ironically, companies striving to keep costs down end up costing the business far more than the costs they were trying to avoid in the first place.

Why? Because current paradigms are so focused on front-end costs and *Preferred Supplier Lists (PSLs)*, which leads to reacting under pressure when talent hasn't been secured by spending quadruple what they were trying to save by bringing consultancies in to rectify the problem.

Sadly, they still fail to find the right talent because of their initial lack of clarity over core requirements, (plus a number of other consultancy-based issues which keep them in the problem rather than resolve it).

Sadly, the rise of procurement has exacerbated this issue of front-end decisions creating back-end problems. And it will continue doing so, unless companies adopt a different approach. One which invests time and money up front in order to save time and money down the line.

Because, what's the real cost of average capability? What's the real cost of compounded mis-hires?

As well as the obvious cost to the company of lost business opportunities and failed programmes, there are hidden costs of damaged morale and demotivation. After all, the right hires are assets, whilst the wrong hires are problem-generators.

This is a massive hidden cost that is rarely mentioned or analysed. Think about it.

How much management overhead do you create when inviting sub-par resource into your business?

It is such a shame that organisations today don't consider the impact of the wrong hires on the right hires.

By bringing in the wrong people, the right people end up leaving. Many people I interviewed explained to me that consultancies often came in and alienated the top 10% who got frustrated and left.

Sadly consultancies can be too schooled in their thinking to change, but more about them later.

Further costs include lost trust in leadership credibility, loss of good people who leave as a result, and the cost of buyers remorse, which often leads to more bad decisions. Cost upon cost.

Oh, the irony.

Mistake 4. Hiring a Recruitment Process Outsourcer (RPO)

Knowledge work is critical to the success of an organisation. So why would you outsource that?

If people are your greatest asset, why outsource a key action that is imperative to the health of your company?

At *Sullivan & Stanley*, we advise never to outsource the ownership of your recruitment entirely. Work with partners by all means and outsource low-end transactional work, but don't hand over ownership of knowledge work to a third party without some retention.

Transferring your recruitment processes to an external service provider when it comes to such mission-critical talent makes no sense and yet so many organisations hand this over to *Recruitment Process Outsourcing (RPO)* firms, along with their blue-collar and cleaning and administrative staff requirements.

I am categorically against companies outsourcing to an *RPO* for a number of reasons.

Knowledge workers should be seen as part of your internal consulting force. As such, you need to retain ownership of their recruitment.

However, from my interview sessions with CIOs it became apparent that those companies who focused on developing in-house on-site HR capabilities, thinking it would be the panacea to all their talent problems, soon discovered they didn't have the IT/change capability to effect change positively.

Furthermore, with HR focusing on cost-saving as a priority, this strategic misalignment rears its ugly head once more. Add to that the fact that recruitment agencies are simply not investing time into clients or candidates any more – at a time when it's really needed, and we have a huge growing problem.

Also, given that '70% of *Fortune 500* CEOs are seeing themselves as technology companies', according to *Forbes*, this requires a different type of individual.

One that is agile, one that is proactive, one that has got a different breadth of skills, can take extreme ownership, and can fundamentally be a positive influence on your wider business, even after they have left.

We all know that companies need to transform the way they are operating in order to keep up and, ideally, stay ahead of change. So there is going to be certain elements of capability augmentation, just to get the right people in your business to deliver the transformation that you need.

But you cannot outsource that. It's problematic at the best of times trying to source people with the right blend of :

- Hard skills
- Soft skills
- Values
- Behaviours
- Passion to make a difference
- Extreme ownership

Indeed, from my interview sessions, I discovered that *a lack of soft skills required to manage change sufficiently* was a huge problem. Many found themselves hiring on hard skills and firing because the required soft skills didn't pan out; or hiring on track record and firing because of the wrong behaviours and attitudes.

Many found this was due to the huge focus on hard-skills within the corporate setting, which recruitment agency policy is aligned to. They learned through this frustration that soft-skills associated with change and delivery is completely under-estimated.

However, this was only discovered with the benefit of hindsight after multiple mis-hires. If only they had devoted time to discovery around their core needs in the first place.

The type of staff many struggled to find included resilient programme staff; the kind of top talent who are currently entering the Interim market (which is where my model and the title of this book comes in).

Indeed most found it problematic trying to search and find the right blend of people who have the hard skills, soft skills, values and passion to make a difference.

And with the traditional approach it's difficult to guarantee behaviours and attitudes as these areas aren't documented like skills are. The only way to guarantee these is to get to know the people in a network and average recruiters don't and can't do that. So a big mistake currently being made by clients and recruiters alike is misjudging IT/change capabilities needed.

And, given that CVs don't work any more in terms of providing adequate insight into behaviour, mindset and comfort zones, for this level of talent, why pay for CV sifters and why outsource a broken recruitment process to an even further broken process? The different type of individual required today needs a different type of vetting.

So how can you trust in-experienced agencies, with little or no experience in recruiting knowledge workers, to vet people for the new world? Indeed, the current *RPO* model has a lot to answer for.

The *RPO* came to prominence in the mid to late *noughties* and became a common feature during the financial crisis in 2007.

The *RPO* was fueled by the prominence of the role of procurement in people decisions, which had traditionally been in the *Human Resources* camp.

Over the years it feels like the *human* element has been removed and that *resources*, i.e. commodity had been replaced where cost was/is the primary decision success factor for the majority of key recruitment partner decisions.

Historically the larger *FTSE* size type organisations have chosen to tie up their companies to a one size fits all model but, alarmingly, any company with a contractor base of 20+ appears to be the target market for some *RPOs* looking to win market share and bet on the future growth of those companies.

But you only need to attend a networking evening of senior change/transformation executives to gauge the general view of an *RPO* and the damage it can inflict in an organisation in terms of programme slippage, failed delivery, wastage of cost, time, business advantage and, of course, the wrong people coming in and the right people leaving.

In the majority of cases, the attempt at saving money has proven to be a flight too close to the sun. Too many companies are getting burned. But why is this?

In order to get people through the door as cheaply as possible, *RPOs* often make significant cuts in the margin payable to recruitment agencies when they can't deliver. Consequently, some of the best/specialised agencies (or their consultants) have refused to work with them, putting them out of reach for decision makers who are now required to hire exclusively through their firm's designated *RPO*.

Furthermore, top 5% talent boycott going through *RPOs*. And, do you think top 5% talent even bothers going through *RPOs*, anyway?

And, when managers do find a contractor they want, working with the *RPO* often means going through additional layers of bureaucracy that didn't exist when they were dealing with the agency directly.

Recently I experienced a situation with an *RPO* where they couldn't find an Interim business partner for seven months. So this large company was without a key interface between technology and the business and unable to facilitate change and translate requests for seven whole months.

We filled the position in four days and were charged a £500 penalty by the *RPO* for their failure. And the client was also fined £750 for going outside of the process. Face palm.

Another example of the damage the *RPO* model can do was when a fast growing successful insurer was at the start of an incredibly difficult transformation, drawing together 200 disparate businesses and systems into a centralised operating model.

As you can imagine, they were notoriously hard to recruit for and were experiencing cultural carnage. The company really needed battle-hardened Interims to win the hearts and minds of the organisation. Top 5% Interims have the experience and the ability to facilitate the change despite heavy resistance. It was the ultimate recruitment challenge.

It took us a good few months of great work to get to know the culture within this tough change environment and to nail the type of battle-hardened individual who would survive, deliver the outcome and create value. Once we had discovered the perfect fit, we delivered what the business needed.

We had cracked it and it was working. We were helping the business deliver benefit by giving them great well-matched people.

However, a new HR director came in and made a front-end decision to bring in an *RPO* to save cost, but this decision ended up costing the company far more than they could ever save.

Turns out it was categorically the biggest mistake that business, via its board and HR director, has made in the last five years. The extra layer of bureaucracy he brought in, the extra layer of uncertainty has meant that the last 18 months has been quite horrific.

The *RPO* literally banned line manager contact as it wanted to recruit first and prevent other recruiters from speaking to the line managers. Time was wasted as key leaders interviewed poorly vetted candidates and didn't ever get access to the best candidates.

The wrong people going in as a result really impeded business advantage for that business, so much so that the HR director who made the decision was fired.

The sad thing is, this is not a rare case, this is the status quo. Poor front-end decisions around cost are costing clients immeasurably. Such is the impact of the broken value exchange.

Evidently, working with an *RPO* can be unwieldy.

Doing so can limit choice sufficiently that managers complain *RPOs* are largely negating the benefits of hiring Interims in the first place.

The knock on effect, due to operational and business pressures, is that clients then have to find a quick fix, so they have no choice other than to go the consultancy route with a body shopping service of what is left on the bench that tends to be up to ten times the price.

The resulting quandary is that:

- Executives and decision makers struggle to find a partner they can trust, struggle to get talent in volume and feel caught between *RPOs*, internal bureaucracy and consulting firms in a spaghetti of process, mistrust and disappointment.
- Decision makers are under duress to hire and often settle for second best which creates buyer's remorse.
- The candidate experience is at an all-time low. Recruitment firms under margin pressure are piling in graduates with next to no training, in serious volume.
- Candidates rarely trust agents, the experience, or the integrity of opportunities and it feels like a malaise is sweeping the industry I love.
- Many of my trusted Interims avoid applying through *RPOs* and are starting to avoid working for corporates with bureaucracy where delivery seems like a pipe-dream.
- You will not get top 5% talent through old routes to capability.

It's a sad state of affairs. In fact, I haven't found many people who have a positive thing to say about the *RPO* model.

So who is the winner in the industry apart from the *RPO* and consulting firms?

An industry that is meant to serve companies and deliver the best people to suit their needs to them? And what's happened to the personal touch in our industry that allows us to be *worth our weight in gold?*

Short-term thinking at board level needs addressing, and fast, to prevent this mistake, which moves us on to ...

Mistake 5. Busting The Preferred Supplier Myth

When you let procurement and HR choose suppliers and tie you in to agreements that offer zero flexibility and create complacency – you have a problem.

When you have procurement or HR telling you to use a certain *Preferred Supplier List (PSL)*, it reduces your flexibility which causes the mistake of being reactive and hiring under duress, and off we go again on the wheel of misfortune amid the recruitment lottery.

With a process as mission critical as securing the best possible talent you can find – *one-size-fits-all* sourcing models or low margin *PSL* agreements are not going to work. And yet it is these kinds of models that procurement signs you up to.

Why? Because it's easier *for them* to do that.

It's not surprising that this happens given the conflicting agendas over *cost vs value*.

However, it shouldn't be happening, given what is at stake. It's time to bust the preferred supplier myth once and for all.

Ultimately, sponsors are seeking ways to recruit outside of the over-processed *PSL* as it doesn't encourage best-practice. Rather, it leaves you with the *C-Team* to CV sift the best results from adverts or a mine of a database.

Crucially, my best associates and candidates never apply for adverts and don't like their CV on a database.

Food for thought.

When you put your talent hunting into the hands of *a PSL*, the talent pool you are gaining access to, is unlikely to have the talent you want within it.

Add another layer of bureaucracy, plus recruitment portals and on-site administrators and you get a really turgid process, which creates in-efficiency and frustration.

Essentially, when you go down this route, you open the door to average people being injected into your organisation at a time when you really need the best people.

But the best people aren't there.

Let's examine this a little closer.

Allow me to take you on a guided tour behind the doors of a recruitment agency. Because it is likely to look a lot different from what you might expect. I know this to be true, because I worked for some of the best in the business for a number of years.

Picture the scene: a large company has a big demand for a multitude of skillsets on a contract and permanent basis. They engage with current suppliers, and invite current and new potential suppliers to submit their tenders for review. Between two and four suppliers are selected to join the *Preferred Supplier List*.

The agency celebrates and announces the win.

However, *because they have compromised so massively on price* in order to secure the deal, *they cannot motivate their best people*.

So they take a team of in-experienced resourcers to source the requirements by posting adverts and CV sifting.

The truth is: *the lower the margin, the less experience*. Again: *to cut the price you have to cut quality or quantity - or both*.

So by saving money you will be left with less-experienced resources to work on your opportunities, both in the larger, medium and smaller agencies.

Welcome to the *C-Team recruitment lottery*.

But where are the *A-Team*?

They're out generating new business and building their own networks. They are new business hunters and prefer to work direct with the client.

Consequently, the majority of *PSLs* are inefficient because they do not and cannot supply you with the expertise you deserve.

That said, to balance the view, the model can work: if it is kept lean and focuses on building trusted relationships.

For example, I have also been a part of successful *PSLs*, where the organisations have realised that the best way to work is to sign up just one or two suppliers and allow them to build relationships with the key decision makers and deal direct.

On the whole, the agent is motivated, can build the relationships needed to be successful and can encapsulate the culture and preferences of the clients at a much deeper level. The result is the organisation's chances of success, agency motivation and access to the best candidates when you need them increases.

Where *PSLs* fall down is when you bloat the process.

Decision makers into HR, into an on-site recruitment agent who then brings in a recruitment portal and signs up the *PSL* agents on a low margin.

This just does not work.

It's a front end *cheap* decision which has a negative impact on the *back-end*. That means *costs*.

Quite simply, it's not good for corporate health, morale or competitive advantage.

And it ends up more expensive.

THE INTERIM REVOLUTION

Mistake 6. Entering The Recruitment Lottery
In The First Place

There is an increasing uncertainty and general feeling of gambling on hires via inflexible culprits i.e., the *PSL* and *RPO* models – detailed here.

Entering into this recruitment lottery in the first place is a mistake.

Many people I interviewed felt like they were playing *Russian Roulette* as a result of reacting to situations rather than responding to needs.

This reactivity-over-proactivity, coupled with allowing inexperienced people to vet and source their candidates through low-cost/value *PSL* and *RPO* models, led to multiple mis-hires.

"It feels like recruitment is a black art", said one interviewee.

Unfortunately, recruitment has become a lottery of winning some (hires) and losing some, creating frustration and mistrust.

However, clients are caught in a trap between agencies supplying them with poorly vetted CVs, line managers laden with over-interviewing, and one big broken process.

And, when it comes to sourcing valuable partners, it's difficult to cut through the red tape of big company processes in order to on-board a new partner quickly. *"It's such a pain to procure good services,"* said one CIO I spoke to.

Unfortunately, despite their best efforts getting them into their current mess, many companies are sticking to the *PSL/RPO* model, because they can't find a route out.

Yet, this means they are gambling on quality hires, stuck with the same recruitment lottery resourcing, same pool and, sadly to say, the same complacency.

So what is a well-intentioned executive to do?

Part of the solution is to find a trusted partner to work in true partnership with. Someone who can truly deliver the talent that will help navigate the change this new world is calling for. With a trusted partner you are no longer gambling on quality hires or entering the recruitment lottery.

However trusted partners can be as difficult to find as change friendly top talent, given the current state of the contractor market. When it comes to sourcing elite candidates, it makes sense to find a partner who adds the personal touch.

Yet, sadly, many of those interviewed said they felt like most companies they engaged with had lost that personal touch. It felt like volume was the prime denominator, which pitched *cost vs quality* and *clients vs agencies*.

The result is a broken matrix of HR, on-site recruitment, *RPO,* a myriad of agencies and consultancies vying for need and the board quibbling over a couple of hundred of quid yet over-spending £200 million in the change portfolio.

Mistake 7. Falling into The Expensive Consultancy Pyramid Trap

The knee-jerk reaction of poor hires is to go to the consulting market, which has seen a proliferation of consulting firms, but this can create even more complex problems.

But why?

If you get what you pay for, surely, it's worthwhile spending a little more by hiring a consultancy to source your capability?

You would think so.

However, after interviewing people who have used consultants, the consultancy market is leaving a bad taste in the mouths of many, because there is a sense of them having their own misaligned agenda.

This agenda is fueled by profit over purpose.

As such, consultancies tend to be in it for the money not the service; they operate primarily to enable their own business to thrive, rather than their clients' business.

The result is often that the client is kept in the problem as the consultancy sells in the *A-Team* to land and expand, whilst iteratively swapping in the *B* and *C-Team*.

In some cases, giving you graduates, who learn on your watch.

Of course, some consulting firms and some recruitment agencies are brilliant. Some have the right values and genuinely want their clients to succeed.

However, if you attend an executive networking event and ask the group their views on consulting, *body-shopp*ing and recruitment agencies, you will most likely hear a similar narrative to the flow of this chapter.

Furthermore, when they do come in, those interviewed frequently reported a worrying lack of alignment. Indeed, many felt that consultancies weren't aligned with the wider business which created conflict and attrition. They felt that management consultants don't tend to bother to get into the behaviours and cultural alignment between the consultants and company.

For these companies, Interim solutions felt more viable.

It's a real shame that even the more costly services are not giving value. Such disparity between cost and value is one of the key problems that causes frustration in the IT/Change flexible workforce market.

What's more, consulting methods tend to be quite outdated, rigid and not particularly responsive, especially when it comes to *body-shopping* i.e. when consultancy firms recruit IT workers to contract their services out on a short-term basis.

Sadly, as a result of the aforementioned list of mistakes that are prevalent in the industry, frustration mounts, programmes and projects slip and, when companies realise they don't have the capability, they hire in consulting firms for things they shouldn't be hiring them for.

Asking a large consultancy firm to *bodyshop* because you haven't got the talent at five times the price is a huge false economy. Far less costly to get the process right first time by planning well and getting the right trusted partners in.

Of course, you've seen it all before.

As these seven mistakes prove, what is needed is something you haven't seen before.

A new, more agile, responsive and smart way of recruiting top talent for those who are really serious about closing their capability and speed gaps so that *Private Equity (PE)* companies, the city, investors, company boards and shareholders can readily align their paradigms to pivot into the new world.

The Agility and Ability Solution

Companies want and need to be agile, but, because of extensive *people-debt*, they can't.

So what can be done?

Most organisations get the wrong side of the equation in the pivot point between agency and consulting firm. There is either the high cost consultancy or the lower cost agency with nothing in the middle.

I believe there is a real opportunity for the recruitment and consulting industry to pivot to where they should be such as towards the centre.

I've been calling this and talking to candidates about it for years and everyone agrees. Nobody I've revealed my solution to disagrees.

Companies want quality resource quickly, mobilised in groups, thoroughly vetted and trusted, but they also want a solution involving a dab or risk and skin in the game.

This is why the solution for the future of recruitment and consulting, as I see it, is this:

A hybrid fusion of the best of Interim management/ consultancy and the best of agency services, to occupy this white space in the middle. This solution enables a trusted partner to provide the right vetted quality groups of people at the right time deployed for an outcome.

Let me explain.

On one side we have the current low margin recruitment agency world which involves *RPOs* and *PSLs*, which generally aren't fit for purpose.

The low cost service and consequential low value creates a recruitment lottery where you gamble on your talent outcome; win some, lose more.

As a result of this mixture of poorly vetted CVs, average candidates *oiked* from a database and over-interviewing, time is wasted and outsourcing to a bloated bureaucratic process pulls on the already-stretched resources and leads to an opportunity cost miss for the business.

As we've defined, this route leads to a widened capability and speed gap which impedes the business performance and level of competitiveness, agility and ability to deliver projects, products, services and progress.

Having already spent out on failed recruitment, decisions are then made that focus on reducing cost rather than reducing failures.

Price punks value and procurement then signs people to a one-size-fits-all model, detrimental to the whole organisation, not just as a result of failed programmes, but as a result of damaged company spirit. It's tough to come back from that.

But it is that which is the norm in so many companies today.

Subsequently, the company reaches out to a consulting firm, on the other side of the equation, paying eight times the price for a *body-shopp*ing service that is simply way too expensive for the value it brings.

For, on this side of the equation, we have high cost services delivering medium value, zero change ownership (as the consultancy is doing all the work) and growing frustration caused by graduates learning on the job as the consulting firms move from using their *A-Team* of best people to secure the business and the *C-Team* of people who are on their backbench to deliver the service.

The pyramid pressure of *body-shopping* then keeps you in a continuous state of problems and you're offered another *Powerpoint* presentation to find a way out.

It's neither agile nor enabling.

Indeed, a pervasive comment from my network has been that they have *had enough of paying that kind of money for consulting firms to tell me the time.*

Mistrust has increased and we are now even seeing organisations banning the use of management consultancies.

I've also heard many horror stories about *Pure Play* consulting, too. This part of the *transformation sector* seems to be doing handsomely well out of the complex ambiguous landscape we find ourselves in.

Where there's mystery, there's margin.

People are lonely and confused. They are lonely at the board and senior leadership team level, because of the pressure they face to solve problems, perform and transform.

On top of that, they've got boards telling them they've got to innovate, so where do they go to? Who do they trust?

Do they go to recruitment firms? Do they go to *Gartner* for advisory? Do they go to *Deloitte* for strategy and people? That's the existing eco-system for the decision-makers to choose from.

Of course, for the huge *big bang* programmes, where you need to source hundreds of people and wish to underwrite the risk, pure play consultancies may be worth pursuing as a solution. But, for the most part, the higher cost consultancy model is as broken as the lower cost agency model.

And so here we are engaged in a race that nobody wins. All of which, I feel is totally avoidable with the right partner, good planning and well-considered process.

Surely there must be something in between?

Another way.

A less frantic way.

A way that suggests that, before we take another step in the wrong direction, we just stop. And we pause.

A reasonably-priced model where value is prioritised?

A framework which boosts agility and ability rather than impedes it?

What people need is the right people, at the right time, with the right support, the right cultural alignment, the right behaviours, at the right price to make shift happen.

A partner who can solve problems and improve capability, giving you the ability to have agility.

In order to get certainty in an uncertain market, there needs to be a focus on building and hiring in recruitment services/ partners who focus on planning and alignment to deliver top quality agile teams and maximum value (and do this with you, in co-ownership).

Future leaders need a future type of change agent.

You need specialists to vet those mindsets, and behaviours; to provide you with certainty, loyalty, speed of action and a solution tailored to help you deliver change.

Something certainly needs to be done. Changes need to be made. A new methodology is desperately needed to ensure that people are not just commoditised but prioritised.

Unfortunately, (and this is difficult for me to write, given that I have worked agency-side for the past 15 years and have worked for two of the better quality technology and change recruitment firms) the industry has never been under so much threat, with the growing trend to cut out the middle man and commoditise talent.

This is what is starting to proliferate:

- Online recruitment dotcom platforms like such as *hired, upwork, reflik, toptal* and *MBACO* are springing up creating a pool of vetted talent.
- The internal recruitment agency is a growing trend. More organisations are starting to develop the full competency internally like *Burberry Executive Search*. However this does not solve all the issues.
- The rush to commoditise the provision of people has created lower margins (and lower quality service), heightened pressures on agencies, top recruitment talent leaving the industry altogether.
- The general state of training, regulation and standards in the recruitment and consulting industry is generating lots of negative energy.
- The rise of procurement in decisions based on a *one-size-fits-all* model is failing.

Consequently, there is a real disparity in the quality of agents and agencies these days. Personally, from building a recruitment company from five people to 120 people, I can vouch first hand for the lack of talent with the right values system I would be looking for in today's market.

My fear is that this powder keg of variables will lead to the disintermediation of the recruitment industry over the next five to ten years. Because, apart from a handful of brilliant head-hunters and agencies out there, where is the real value in today's recruitment business'?

The top 20% will also survive, adapt, fall into a niche or a premium spot but what about the others?

In five years' time will organisations really want to pay for *body-shopping* or CV sifting service, one with no co-ownership or skin in the game?

What are agencies currently doing to get ahead of the curve? Are we speaking to our customers to find out what they really want? Are we building more value around the process?

Are we in the boards business plan as a real key provider of talent on demand? Do we have a trusted relationship with the key decision makers or is it a transactional, portal driven, account manager, CV transaction?

The result of this status quo is the perpetuation of a *recruitment lottery*, and today, more than ever before, good talent is not something any company should be gambling on.

So, what's the solution?

Done well, I believe there is a powerful intersection between *Interim leaders* and *top 5% recruiters – network builders.*

If the future is about communities and engaging with them, (which is a real passion of mine) there is no one better than a recruiter who is personally focused on sourcing the best top 5% individuals and curating them into an active network.

That's where the opportunities exist.

By planning effectively to create positive processes that enable companies to find the right partner, talented teams can be delivered who will not only make change programmes successful, but will leave their mark on the organisation by sharing their values and knowledge with existing teams.

For it's my belief that organisations will become more fluid, network based squads - constantly in a state of change. Organisations need a different type of skill-set which requires a more in-depth vetting process. As such, I believe that a hybrid solution (a hybrid of Interim leaders and top 5% recruiters) is the different approach that the industry so desperately needs.

A hybrid that will provide a trusted partner who will devote sufficient time to discovery, planning and alignment in order to deliver pre-gelled teams who can bolster capability fast, deliver business value at pace and boost agility to win the war on talent and deliver change better and faster than ever before.

That's how we do enable agility. By running engaging communities that we can tap into to find the right people at the right time. That's the movement we're starting and it's my vision to take this global.

Key Takeaways

- A mismatch of objectives between what leaders and executives want (good talent); what HR/procurement/finance want (cost savings); and what agencies want, (access to decision makers); has created a broken value exchange that needs to be replaced with a happy value chain.
- Successful companies don't outsource their strategy; they don't outsource ownership of change.
- One size *does not* fit all. Don't hire an RPO. You need separate trusted partners and processes in place to provide instant access to knowledge workers, niche capability and a bespoke solution that works for you.
- You get what you pay for. *Focus on quality.*
  Spending less *is* a false economy. Average capability costs in terms of morale, lost opportunities and failed programmes. But don't fall into the consultancy trap and lose ownership of change.
- Mistakes cost. Be careful about what front end decisions you are making and the back end results that you're getting. Poor front end decisions can ruin your business or cost years of business advantage. You can no longer afford to make such costly mistakes. The new world is *not* forgiving.

Rapid Action Points

- Think about your current models of sourcing. Are you really struggling with interview debt? How many of your most recent hires were made under duress, reactively? Be honest.
- Analyse the strength of your resource pool. Have you genuinely got top 5% resources? Are you paying market rates for the best? Is top 5% even a priority?
- What would top 5% look like to you - exactly?

- Trial a project where you augment with top 5% only. Remember hiring three *A-Players* trumps hiring ten average cost-prioritised *C-Players*. Are you prioritising cost or value?
- Do you have a policy that even supports top 5%? What changes do you now need to make with your recruitment processes to create a happy value chain?
- What can you do *today* to ensure recruitment certainty rather than recruitment uncertainty?
  - Seek a new partner
  - Factor in better planning
  - See knowledge-workers as part of your internal consulting force
  - Go where the best people are
  - Prioritise people and prevent procurement from choosing low-value, low-margin suppliers
- Plan and align. Be proactive, not reactive. Respond, don't react when determining and defining your core needs: hard and soft skills, values, behaviours, role requirements, business vision.
- Know what *good* looks like for your organisation. Take the time to really understand your needs. Map it out carefully and put people, capability and talent at the heart of your agenda.
- Prioritise trusted partnerships with those who offer a personalised service and people who can vet for the new world; who are motivated to build relationships and work with you to ensure good results.
- Look where you can cut waste and bureaucracy in RFP, tenders, onboarding, paperwork and decision-making.
- Measure time to hire.
- If you want to be an agile organisation, be agile with your sourcing and onboarding.

Chapter 4

A Fresh Perspective and New Model
For Change – The Interim Teams Revolution

Chapter 4:
A Fresh Perspective and New Model For Change – The Interim Teams Revolution

*"One of the biggest things in business
is to open yourself up for change."*
Jay Z, *Musician and Record Label Boss*

Agile At Scale

In business, in order to get from where you are now to where you need to be, in order to quicken the pace of delivery and close the speed gap, conventional processes must be rethought and reinvented to become more agile at scale.

That's the premise of this book and the model it presents – agility, alignment and access to the best available resource; to close the capability gap and win that war for talent.

Becoming agile and nimble at scale enables enterprises to remain competitive in an ever-changing world. Yet, it can only happen by simplifying IT estate and recruitment processes, aligning with strategy and developing a culture of agility across the business at large.

Because, when it comes to rapid scalability, simplicity is the key ingredient of agility.

Harnessing technology to simplify processes is one way to make your organisation more agile.

However, another core effective way to become more agile at scale, stay lean and fill the capability and speed gaps is by bringing in agile talent to supplement your existing permanent staff and boost capabilities within the fast-paced strategic areas of the business, team by team, product by product.

The great thing about agile talent is that each individual is performing (or should I say out-performing) mission-critical tasks at their uppermost top level in squads. The impact this can have on the company is tremendous. And just imagine the impact the combination of those minds would have when they are hired as part of an agile team?

One of our company motto's is: *a hand-picked team for every meaningful mission.*

Bringing in the best expertise on tap is dependent on a number of factors.

You need to find the right tap to make the talent flow such as partners who can find the right talent.

You also need to nurture relationships with those partners and you need to generate clear and simple processes that enable you to communicate how projects are planned and implemented.

As such, you need alignment between who you work with, how you work and why you work (and source) that way.

You also need to be responsive enough to *sense and respond* rather than *plan and predict*. This requires the allocation of discovery time, and the right collection of mindsets.

Organisations that tap into the most agile, Interim talent tend to be purposeful companies that exceed customer expectations. They do this by building an agile army of talent, testing often, measuring and aligning constantly and enabling autonomy and agility at scale without letting bureaucracy slow them down or take away their start-up mindset.

These are the companies of the future.

Examples include *Pandora, Spotify, Netflix* and *AirBnB.*

They devote time to constant discovery and delivery.

But there's something else that these companies do.

By tapping into the collective minds of autonomous teams and having an agile response to embracing change, these companies are not only enabling innovation, they are also *future proofing* their operations so that they may thrive, consistently so.

In fact, companies organised this way are only ever two weeks away from correcting any mistakes.

So, we know that we need to source trusted partners who can supply agile talent and have aligned processes and dedicated systems in place to maximise the performance of such talent.

But how do we ensure success and minimise uncertainty, given the rapid rate of change and strategic imperative of the task at hand?

We can do this by exploring and choosing a fresh model that harnesses a hybrid of the best recruitment and consulting practices to source the best possible talent and deliver the best possible outcomes.

A Hybrid Recruitment/Consultancy Solution – Presenting The Interim Teams Revolution

It's well known in the industry that the top 5% recruiters can find incredible people on an Interim basis and generate sales like no other.

If you mix that ability with the power of agile Interim talent – that's a powerful intersection that enables superior talent acquisition and increased efficiency. Ultimately then, if you intersect Interims and brilliant recruiters with business problems in a triangle, you can accrue some stunning gains.

It's easy to harp on about the best possible talent, but we all know that the risks and costs involved in discovering the top permanent staff have long been high, so why should placing temporary staff be any different?

Well, I am pleased to tell you that there is a solution.

Imagine if you could access *A-Listers* on-demand?

My twist on that is, rather than hire only individual Interims into your organisation, you work with a trusted partner who enables a *Team of Interims* to crowd around a problem to deliver key outcomes.

They then disperse onto the next assignment, but not before positively impacting your organisation and leaving behind some critical components of their expertise and knowledge that can be retained by your organisation.

The paradigm shift is to see Interim knowledge workers, leaders and super coaches there, to help your organisation evolve.

This model is similar to how a casting director would make a movie in Hollywood.

The problem with pulling teams together is that the status quo has created a world of poor processes, poor alignment between behaviours and cultures and poor partner choice.

However, if these three areas can be nailed, pre-packaged teams offer a viable solution.

And, if the recruiter can become a trusted partner by getting rid of the old broken processes and, instead, providing a genuinely appealing new process; one which focuses on trust and alignment and quality delivery, all of those mistakes uncovered could be resolved.

As such, the future of people provision could be bright rather than murky.

Consequently, the *Interim Revolution* and model I've created is a fresh perspective on recruiting, advisory and consulting, suited to any organisations pro-active around changing and flexing to the new world (or to organisations who just simply have to change to survive).

It's a model that encompasses trusted sourcing, trusted consulting, and advisory-on-demand to provide trusted transformation.

Why Interims?

Interim management has played a major role in my recent business life. Since placing my first Interim IT Director and Change agent many years ago, I have been fascinated by the spirit of a true Interim professional.

They are a *gun for hire* to help companies deliver, solve problems, make sense of technology and coach/improve everyone who comes into contact with them.

The Interim Management market sprung out of strict labour laws in the 1980s Netherlands where it became prohibitively costly to hire or fire permanent staff. Experienced executives were brought in during crises or to manage an organisation as a whole, manage change or implement strategic actions.

Since the 2008 recession, the concept has taken off in America and now more and more elite executives are entering the Interim talent pool market, to leverage and benefit from their own expertise within more rewarding and flexible working environments, both Stateside and in the UK.

I've been fortunate enough to have an insiders insight into why so many top quality executives are leaving secure roles to enter the Interim market.

So please allow me to open my agency door again and illustrate a typical meeting I might have with a typical candidate who has been permanent for over ten years working in an enterprise setting. They've been working the corporate ladder, receiving incremental pay increases, job promotions, working their way up the project/leadership ladder, playing the politics game until, one day, they decide enough is enough.

A portfolio of this typical client's friends are now Interims and so they are aware that, if their friends can do it so could they, given that demand for Interims has never been higher. Many of my clients specifically state they would prefer Interims as they are so frequently of a better quality to permanent.

So, we have a match.

They meet with me for advice on how to get into the Interim market, how to build a network, how to play the agency game and other bits of advice that I'm happy to give. And I always ask them why they are looking to go Interim? What's the draw?

The majority are unanimous that they want a different relationship with their careers. They want more flexibility and they want work with more focus, purpose and intensity. They're growing increasingly disillusioned with executive life.

As individuals, they know they are capable of so much more; they want to add value, solve problems and drive forward; they want to transform the culture, save an organisation that was heading for bankruptcy and make a difference.

As such, *The Interim Revolution* isn't just about what's good for business, it's about what's good for the individual and it's about enabling them to make the most of their own talent.

At the follow up meeting, after I've placed them in their first Interim assignment, the majority of my typical clients feel that they've found their new purpose in life. The allure of focused work, where they can bring their IP/experience to the table and execute in a variety of different organisations, project-by-project, enables them to develop and grow. This is, in part, due to the nature of the variety of different people, situations and problems they've encountered.

Over time they become even more experienced and enjoy the flexibility.

Bringing an elite specialist in for a period of time is the purest form of employment.

In a nutshell, an Interim manager is an experienced, often senior manager who has been hand-picked to match the precise needs of a company and is generally hired for between six to nine months. They should not be confused with consultants, because they don't just advise, they deliver too.

Implementation is the key. As is simplicity. Advisory, coaching and delivery are the key hallmarks of a decent Interim and the experience and honesty is well worth the price.

Contracts for hiring Interims are less complex and simpler than those for hiring their permanent counterparts. What's more, remove extra costs such as *National Insurance* (NI) contributions, bonuses, pension, company car benefits that are often added to a permanent executive's salary, and it's easy to see that the perception around Interim management being more expensive couldn't be further from the truth.

Moreover, management becomes easier and less complex too.

So, rather than manage talent, managers can focus on managing results and outcomes. The future is all about access to talent, not ownership of talent.

Not only that – the benefits are incredibly valuable.

Given the need for speed in today's dynamic business climate, making decisions and responding to opportunities quickly is a must. Interims are ideal for these objectives because they have immediate availability and can consequently make immediate impact on delivery of results. The bottom line, you can respond to opportunities, deliver results much faster with an Interim who is in the business of hitting the ground running, with the added bonus of sufficient knowledge and experience under their belt.

Conversely, it takes new permanent employees a month or more to get started, (up to six months in some cases) as they often need to serve out their notice period. Few permanent staff hand in their notice until they are assured of a new position.

Interim leaders can inject expertise and capability around a variety of disciplines into your organisation instantly; transformation experts can be hired to deliver on a key programme and keep agenda from the board; programme managers, project managers, process people, architects technical analysts, teams of the best in these areas can be sourced and vetted and their knowledge and capabilities harnessed.

Furthermore, Interims are guaranteed to have a proven track record in working on the type of problem or project that your enterprise requires expertise in and/or within a specific sector.

As such, they will be committed to delivering key outcomes and results.

They will have vast knowledge and experience that equips them to deal with challenging issues and can make things happen quickly. This is especially useful when time-frames are tight and requirements are immediate.

They also provide added value, not just by being over-qualified, (thus giving organisations access to experience that would be less affordable if permanent) but also by sharing their expertise internally before moving on to their next assignment.

I love the stories I hear about how Interims have gone in and taken project managers and even leaders under their wing; about how they have shared knowledge and built new courage and capability in them. That is what it is all about these days – helping, collaborating and improving.

This means that their expertise and changes made won't just wither when they go. It will be embedded into the organisation and culture and continue to deliver value, long after they've moved on.

Interims have one objective, *to make maximum impact in a short space of time.* As such, they work hard and they work well.

By working smarter and faster, they cost less – and certainly less than they would if you hired such high calibre individuals on a permanent basis. For Interims, you're only as good as your last assignment, so if you mess up, it's a blot on your paper, hence why Interims tend not to.

Another benefit is, Interims are not bogged down in politics and subsequently cut through the bureaucracy that is stifling the evolution of British business' today.

They won't tell senior team members what they want to hear, but will tell them what they need to hear, because they don't need to dilute their opinions to protect their long-term career aspirations at the firm. They just tell it like it is. Refreshing (and rewarding).

What's more, Interims enable you to take ownership of the changes you make. Henry Cohen, *CIO* says:

> *"A lot of organisations bring in consultancies and the consultancy team comes in and they do the work, so there is no ownership from the client. There is no commitment from the client, because they don't have skin in the game, because the consultancy is doing the work.*
>
> *By having an Interim, an individual, who gets the organisation to own the change, to get skin in the game; that makes the change happen, because it's the organisation doing the change, and the Interim facilitating it."*

It's no surprise that the *guns for hire* market is growing.

When you need to resource a big project, or cope with rapid change, having the ability to inject the company with a specialist resource for a specific time period is golden.

Ultimately, hiring Interims enables you to get your hands on much-needed expertise whilst simultaneously minimising risk. And when you can access those executives on-demand, you can more readily navigate complex situations and gain a competitive edge.

However, I would say that this model is *evolutionary* rather than *disruptive*. It is not about to replace permanent staff; rather it will provide a way for organisations to become more agile and flexible by bringing in agile teams to work alongside their existing employees and add immense value to proceedings.

Indeed, I see this hybrid between recruitment and consulting as the future. Because, when you integrate consultancy with Interim management, you are able to recruit people who can solve problems, manage projects, deliver change and coach/

motivate and engage your existing staff to sustain delivery going forward in co-partnership with you. Interims are over-experienced, have been there before and know what they are doing.

Sadly, the exponential discretionary benefit you get from an engaged Interim professional is underrated in today's business world.

Although the use of Interims is growing fast, according to the *Interim Management Association* (IMA), the use of Interims has grown by 93% since the pre-recession levels of 2006, with the sector tipped to become a £2 billion market.

It's my belief that, with the advent of the *Gig Economy* and the world's changing attitudes towards their work-life balance, the flexible working model is only going to become more popular.

On its own, however, *Interim Management* sometimes struggles to find its voice, because they're traditionally hired in to solve problems or fill a gap, yet this is where organisations need to raise their thinking, because Interims have so much more to offer than problem-solving and gap-filling. As a result they are still under used and under backed.

This is why, at *Sullivan & Stanley*, we're bringing together a community of incredible individuals (top 5% of Interims) to help organisations to change, which, as a group, creates a revolution.

By building communities of these top 5% Interims, doing a lot of relationship building, workshopping and gelling and pre-packacing in the background, through our *Teams as a Service (TaaS)* model, we can create mutually beneficial opportunities for under-used talent and for the organisations who need them.

And it's having some stunning results already.

Opportunities for Interims can be hard to come by in a consultancy dominated advisory environment.

Yet, I believe that the flaws in both the recruitment model and Interim Management resolve when they both intersect.

Recruiters cannot be surplus to requirements if entwined with a good Interim, and Interim Managers can find their voice and opportunities when entwined within the network and sales engine of a good recruiter.

Sullivan & Stanley exists at the intersection of both *recruitment/consultancy* and *Interim Management* to empower global enterprise organisations.

And I am relentlessly curious about exploring new ways to create value for the customer at this intersection.

My view is that recruitment for the independent agency is dying. The future will include self-serving platforms and automated CV-matching by bots and other *AI* platforms.

But the real way to build top 5% recruiters and enable real change is via the curation of temporary teams who cross-pollinate with permanent teams; it's through independents/virtual consulting teams crowding together and working in unison with organisations for exceptional outcomes.

All of which gives the ability to help deliver agility. Because Interims are, by nature, agile.

But there is much more to them than that.

Allow me to reiterate and explore in more detail the core benefits of hiring Interims:

- **Return on investment and value for money.**
  Interim managers aren't paid just to turn up,
  they are paid to achieve objectives and deliver results.
  They harness their deep expertise and skillsets to
  mitigate risk or deliver an outcome and consequently
  generate a significant return on any investment
  in their placement.
- **Immediate availability and results.**
  Speed is a key benefit, given that there is no need to wait
  for them to work out a notice period. As such, they can
  be committed to solving your problems or managing
  rapid change within a matter of days, rather than weeks
  or months.
  They have experience of prompt engagement,
  so can get on with the work quickly and effectively.

- **Wealth of knowledge and experience.**
  The level of expertise Interim managers bring to the
  table (for a fraction of the cost that a permanent
  executive with the same capabilities would cost)
  is second to none. They use this expertise to address
  specific issues and make a positive impact from the
  outset.
- **Objectivity.**
  They are politically distanced from cultural politics,
  so will tell you what you need to know rather than what
  you want to hear. They can therefore cut through the BS
  to focus on whatever is genuinely best for the business.
- **Higher accountability.**
  Interim managers are not consultants or advisors,
  they take responsibility and have accountability for
  the results they are expected to generate as stewards
  of a specific project.
- **Commitment to results.**
  Interim managers effect significant transformation
  because a) their future work depends on a successful
  track record including positive references and referrals
  and b) they have significant authority as executives
  operating near or at board-level, unlike temps who are
  only in place to *hold the fort*. Interims are committed to
  achieving goals and performing to a high standard to
  add significant value and get good results. As such they
  are motivated because they have a stake in the success
  of the projects in which they are involved.

Seizing this opportunity that the surging *Gig Economy*
provides helps close the skills and speed gaps, whilst
simultaneously empowering elite candidates with more
control.

The Interim Revolution is also a conduit for corporates to
become more flexible, like start-ups; more fluid.

Evidently using Interims is a win-win. But hiring a few Interims
compared to a whole collection of Interims? Let's explore that.

A Collection of Minds:
Filling The Gap And Delivering Outcomes
By Crowdsourcing Pre-Gelled Top 5% Teams

It's not just the *Gig Economy* that is providing organisations with huge opportunities, but the shared network economy is also enabling corporations to fill gaps and deliver outcomes by tapping into teams and harnessing a collection of minds.

Indeed, a flexible interconnected *network of teams* is fast becoming the new organisational model of choice.

Business leaders have realised that, by empowering teams to tackle specific challenges and work on particular projects, the holy grail of agility is achievable.

They've discovered that *lean* is within reach.

They've discovered that, as the teams disband and move on to new gigs, they leave behind knowledge that is not only valuable, but sustainable too.

Until now, the talent war problem has had a number of so-called solutions thrown at it; from outsourcing to off-shoring, from poaching talent to racking up the compensation.

The costs of these endeavours have been more than just monetary, as explored in previous chapters.

None of these options have solved the talent war problem in its entirety, hence the need for alternative approaches.

Enter *crowdsourcing* – a fresh way to address the talent issue, which enables organisations to tap into a scalable agile workforce; a carefully curated collective talent pool of highly-skilled, top quality and flexible workers, on-demand.

Because, problems shouldn't be outsourced; a collective of minds can solve any problem.

My view is that leaders need to get the right people around a white board and get a view of what good looks like in six, 12, 18 months; i.e., use teams to create a plan and solution and revisit periodically.

In this ever-changing, human-centric, collaborative and connected world, engaging a crowd of people towards achieving a common goal, is fast-becoming a viable solution to the talent war issue. This is why some innovative companies, especially in the States, are starting to dip their toes into the crowdsourcing pool as a way to alleviate issues and modernise the workforce.

Crowdsourcing provides the enterprise with an elastic talent pool that enables them to source solutions from the best minds in the world, regardless of geography.

Leveraging the *Gig Economy* through a structured crowdsourcing method, I believe, would alleviate some of the pain points with accessing top talent to solve problems, whilst alleviating pressures from burning platforms, *technical and organisation debt* and, of course, *capability and capacity* issues.

I genuinely feel that, if crafted correctly, this is a solution that could impact the talent war and enable access to agile talent, when you want, how you want it, at a price that is fair.

Imagine having access to the world's best minds and experience, culturally aligned to churn through projects at an unprecedented rate, pulled into you on tap, through a trusted partner?

I'm yet to be convinced of some of the online market places, but I think there is a place for a personalised structured hybrid crowdsourcing solution to give enterprise real options and get ahead of the curve.

The way I see it, Interim Team Management fits snugly between the need for alignment and the need for teams.

It's a massively underused yet structured method to procure collective knowledge on tap.

So, let's assume you are totally sold on hiring Interims. How do you best engage with this flexible knowledge workforce to fully maximise the opportunity that this growing on-demand trend presents?

And, given that *Interims-en-masse* are likely to have a more substantial impact on your operations, how do you source top-notch teams of Interims and create certainty when vetting an array of these knowledge workers?

As a result of my passion for exploring alternatives to the recruitment status quo, I have developed a personalised service that can guarantee as many as 250 Interims landing and working effectively to generate strong results whilst saving the client time, as I did with the *Easynet/Sky* integration.

And we all know that time is money, right?

We'll focus more on the model in the following chapter, for now it's important to focus on why teams of Interims may unlock the route to prosperity in this current climate.

Of course, hiring an Interim feels like it's a singular transaction, but that's because it's still tarnished with the recruitment brush.

Furthermore, there is often a disconnect between hiring an individual Interim and the requirement for a team that can work together. A single Interim brought in to work with existing permanent staff is actually less easy than bringing in a pre-gelled team, if it's done correctly.

Another benefit of teams from an Interim's perspective is the *power of unity*.

Being a sole trading Interim can be a lonely spot.

You are just one lone voice; but when you are part of a team, that's energising. That's why we've created *The Change Society*, which is our community of Interims and the first iteration of this revolution.

We're a mobilised crowd of Interims; there's strength in numbers and the Interim movement needs this energy to spark a revolution.

That's why we've curated an invitation-only community of Interim board members and *C-Suite* change agents who've joined together as a virtual consulting pool to crowd around business problems. For, I believe, tapping into a collection minds is far better than tapping into just one.

Enter Stage Left – The Hollywood Model and The Professional Casting Director

The *Teams as a Service (TaaS)* model involves hiring, through a trusted partner, a team of Interims, an agile talent collective; to crowdsource around a problem or opportunity to deliver key outcomes.

Just as a team of talented actors, producers, directors, camera people and engineers all come together to work on a movie project and are paid as a result of a desired outcome, agile Interim teams, come together to work on a change strategy or innovation project, before dispersing.

Importantly, the casting director asks, *who are the best people we can hire for this movie to make it a blockbuster?*

Films are 90% casting, as all directors will tell you.

The same can be said for enterprise. People make all the difference, no matter what industry they work in.

Furthermore, in the same way that the new Hollywood model and the way that movie productions are organised can be used as an analogy for agile teams sourced from a trusted network, the collapse of the big studio institutions that ran Hollywood movie making for so long can be viewed as parallel with what is currently happening to the big corporations. Indeed, many businesses are finding that sheer size isn't the advantage it used to be.

The vast majority of Hollywood movies used to be created by the studio system: huge corporations with massive payrolls and equally imposing bureaucracy, which exerted control over production of as many as 350 movies per year.

Back then, the studio system had centralised management and resources would be efficiently allocated to create the movies; from lighting and camera operators to the actors, directors, set directors and so on.

For a number of reasons, the studios started to decline in the late 1940s and gradually lost their influence over the next few decades. It feels like today's corporates are going through a similar decline.

Some of the big studios like *Sony Pictures* and *20th Century Fox* still exist as large corporations always shall, but they control a much smaller slice of the industry than the Hollywood studios once did.

What thrived as a result of this seismic shift of thinking within Hollywood was a variety of independent companies created for the *on-demand* requirement for each new production.

This approach, where teams of producers secure funds and establish new enterprises to make a specific movie, continues to thrive in today's multi-billion pound film industry. With the funds secured and the company incorporated, they hire the agile teams of personnel and subcontractors; including the director, leading actors, accountants and caterers, and use talent agencies to effectively matchmake the talent for the production team.

These small independent producers with their temporary networks of brilliant people were able to create more attractive productions than the traditional big studios, at a fraction of the cost. The studios struggled against these new independent and agile producers. The emergence of this new networked industry led to more innovative productions.

Films like *Resevoir Dogs* and *Pulp Fiction*, simply would not have been made within the old traditional studio system.

This network organisation gave much more freedom to talented directors to create movies that they wanted to direct, and for talented actors to play the roles they wanted to play.

Today it's possible for both actors and directors to work on blockbuster movies alongside their work on independent films. Doing so provides much more career satisfaction and also generates higher quality and increased innovation within the film industry.

People are given the freedom to follow their own dreams and ambitions, which raises the bar of delivery and execution as everyone is engaged and focused.

The new role of the recruiter will be similar to firms like *10xmanagement.com* is and my own *Sullivan & Stanley* firm, whereby recruiters are essentially network builders and connectors, curating tight talent pools with a process to assemble great teams to deliver outcomes, just like Hollywood matchmakers connect the talent and movie producers.

In this way, the recruiter becomes the casting director.

Hollywood, as an industry, has evolved because of its move towards a more agile model of connected networks and the sourcing of professional teams of individuals whose sources of income vary. Today, the movie industry is in a strong position, as a result of the *power lunches* that Hollywood is renowned for; all that networking has created a *tightly woven web of relationships that help connect talent with those who need it.*

As Hollywood has proven, size isn't everything after all. Hence why various other industries are going through similar experiences to the collapse of the studio system.

The *big bang* approach to large programmes is clearly not the most innovative or cost effective way of delivery; nor are industrial command and control style organisations as efficient as they would hope to be.

Sometimes, the only way to hire the best talent is on a contract basis. The unpredictable nature of business in this emergent world means that hiring and continuously staffing a dedicated team, isn't always the best method. As such, companies need to challenge their thinking and look for future models to help them stay innovative and competitive.

Frankly, your best thinking from three years ago is your biggest baggage today.

Increasing numbers of professionals (as highlighted earlier) are realising that they are opposed to working for the same company for years, in the same rigid structure, hoping for a promotion, frustrated by lack of delivery/innovation and draconian leadership behaviours.

The world is happening and unfolding outside and it's never been easier, with the age of new technology, to bravely venture out on your own, become an Interim and get amongst the revolution of focused, purposeful work, on your terms.

Most of the people I have met are now Interims and have made the leap to a portfolio Interim journey. They realised they can maximise their earning potential and choose the work they really want to do, for the companies they would like to partner with to create value and deliver outcomes. They are choosing a journey, freedom, experience and choice over job security and careers.

And it's getting easier.

In response to the growing numbers of freelance professionals, there are more tools available, which are disrupting and simplifying the process of collecting invoices, paying a group of Interims and tracking expenses. And it is so easy now to find flexible office space and avoid the corporate noose of a multi-year office lease.

What's more, whether it's Hollywood power lunches, Shoreditch business breakfasts, or online networks that we frequent, we are more enabled than ever before to get to know more people and have them get to know us, so that we may build relationships and develop connections and, in doing so, find work and people to work with us.

All of this means that people are enabled to find work outside of the traditional permanent employment model and employers are enabled to find agile talent outside of traditional recruitment models.

Consequently, for me, there is no reason for professionals and companies to stick with what's got them to where they are today.

Organisational design is being challenged as the Hollywood studio system was decades ago.

Many US companies are starting to recognise this and premium recruitment agencies are beginning to thrive through a model of connecting the best to the best and offering a *team curation service*.

In the US we are even seeing superstar tech engineers being represented by agents, just like movie stars. It's a growing trend and one which savvy companies and elite talent are riding with.

In and around industry, there are green shoot signs that working teams will soon be a lot like movie crews.

And there's no denying that *handpicking* and *curating* an elusive high-performance team, pre-packaged together from a trusted crowd to deliver an outcome, is an attractive proposition; teams that will get you out of a problem, solve it, disperse and also leave you with internal benefit and significant gain for your core perm team.

This paradigm shift will challenge some, but I truly believe in my Irish bones that this contract/Interim industry is the future of work: a genuine solution in dealing with emergent change and a genuine alternative to consulting firms, who can cause so much confusion, frustration and *organisational debt*.

As the evolution of Hollywood demonstrates, the collapse of the studio system did not put an end to incredible films, inspirational stars and wonderful parties.

Far from it in fact. Hollywood is thriving via the power of freelance teams.

And, just as the best stars (both in front of and behind the camera) want to work on the best films, so too does the best talent across any industry want to work on the best projects. A gig portfolio enables them to do exactly that, they have the choice to do what they truly want to do, gain much more experience on the journey and focus on delivering value. As such, I can't think of a similar model that would solve so many of today's business problems if adopted.

The modern firm is much more focused on managing changes and innovating. This shift is where industry is now; it's all about solving complex problems rather than managing standard tasks. Hence why most organisations are essentially a collection or portfolio of projects – projects which teams can come in and tackle and excel in delivering the required outcome.

The Importance of Alignment, Process and Partners

The future is teams. The problem with trying to put teams together is an inability to get alignment. But why is that?

In my experience, this is partly due to poor processes and partly due to poor partners.

But mainly this comes from the perpetual cycle of misalignment which stems from poor planning. That acts as the catalyst for this never-ending loop.

So, at first, people aren't planning, they're reacting, which means they don't have or put adequate processes in place to recruit effectively, so they end up making poor front end decisions and choosing the wrong partners.

This, in turn, creates further misalignment between what they actually need and what they end up with, and so it goes on – reacting instead of planning, making poor decisions around partners and failing to put the right processes in place that would enable them to step out of this unfortunate loop.

Consequently, one thing leads to another to create *a chain of continual misalignment.*

Each time the wrong decision is made as a result of poor planning, you end up with the wrong partner with the wrong processes, all of which puts the organisation under too much stress.

It's a misalignment nightmare.

Over time, having interviewed hundreds of executives, change agents and candidates, success comes down to three key things that you need to have, but which corporates rarely do.

- **Alignment** - to reduce the capability and speed gap
- **Process** - to reduce the capability and speed gap
- **Trusted Partner** - to secure great people and teams to tackle the new worlds' challenges

When you can tick the box of all three of these, you get great results when sourcing the right people and on-boarding project teams effectively.

However, it's no good having two out of three of these right; you need all three in order to succeed at recruiting, and, if you have a poor partner, game over.

I've seen poor decisions being made despite having gone in and achieved great alignment.

I've been in a position where alignment is good, the sponsors are trusting the process, we've got to know the culture and personalities and have a strong understanding of what type of people are needed.

Then, all of a sudden, an executive makes the decision to bring in an *RPO* and boom. We're back to square one.

You need alignment, slick processes and a trusted partner in order to achieve what is needed to survive in today's ever-changing business climate.

For example …

Value-Added Rapid Results On Demand

I've always designed successful transformation teams iteratively and it's worked, as the *Easynet/Sky* integration and *Burberry* case studies below reveal.

Now, though, I've put my IP into the process to create *Teams as a Service (TaaS)* and we have delivered pre-packaged teams for other companies, two of which we'll explore here.

My experience with *Easynet/Sky* and *Burberry* helped me to define what worked and what was needed when I was developing the *TaaS* model.

My experience with the companies I've worked with since founding my own business, prove that *TaaS* really works.

I've always been relentlessly curious about exploiting value around building teams, which is why I enjoyed building teams for the *Easynet/Sky* integration and building teams with *Burberry.*

There were some common denominators around how and why I was able to do my best work before launching *Sullivan & Stanley* and since developing our teams model, all of which has enabled me to place the right people at the right time with the right behaviour/cultural alignment for the right price, and fast. That is a service!

And that is a service that I am bringing to the world.

Environment was conducive to the success of these projects.

In the late *noughties*, I had the pleasure of sourcing 250 Interims and 45 *Permanent project workers* especially for the integration of *Easynet/Sky* and we had a 90% success rate.

We did this without wasting any time or money and without losing business focus or putting the organisation under considerable interview burden.

Rather, we executed a strategic plan to bring in *DSL* skills and equipped *Easynet* by head-hunting an amazing *DSL* team.

When you get alignment, you can discover the best solution, set the process, timeline and deliver results on demand. As the *Easynet/Sky* integration proves, this can be done at scale.

Similarly, at *Burberry*, the project mandate required the placement of an Interim leadership team and each one of those Interim leaders had their own mandate to deliver.

Burberry did not have the capability in-house and did not want to draw upon their vendor resource pool.

They needed a *capability accelerator*; a hand-picked crack team of the best from the market who would be loyal to what they wanted to get done in a defined space of time, before looking to replace with permanent staff.

Essentially, *Burberry* needed six to 12 month injection of expertise to achieve business outcome, and it was a roaring success. That capability helped put technology and digital at the heart of their strategy.

These solutions gave minimal interview overheads and had a 100% stick rate of resources.

After establishing *Sullivan & Stanley,* we worked with the CIO of a *Global Enterprise Service Provider (Company X under NDA)* to rapidly assemble a problem-solving recovery team and deliver on innovation for the board, all within two weeks.

They had two missions:

1. A rescue mission to turn around an underperforming IT services department and transform that capability, whilst
2. Freeing up that executive to own the innovation agenda and develop a digital shift strategy to pitch to their board and investors

This is a situation that many of today's CIO/CTOs face.

Technical debt, bloated IT departments, legacy systems, but with pressures from the board to digitise and create, own and deliver on the innovation agenda.

Our *Teams as a Service* process was able to get a crack unit team to work with the CIO, resolve the former whilst freeing up space to deliver on the latter and guide that in partnership with the CIO. Both teams were successful for that executive and both teams were high-performing.

Another example of the imperative need to work with clients in partnership, is our work with the UK's largest payment provider, *(Company Y)*, a traditional financial services company which had endured years of management consultancies failing to deliver anything of substance.

This company had disparate regional businesses dotted around the country and had rejected many vendors and consulting firms over the years as the projects and/or change were delivered *to* them, as opposed as a partner *with* them.

The current technology executive had been pitching an idea to the new CEO in order to transform their operating model from a traditional service operation based business to a faster, more responsive, product based company. As such, what was needed was a full scale business agility transformation with continuous delivery at the heart of the technology engine.

Our brief was to enable them to pivot quickly, become more efficient, effective and shorten the delivery cycles for their products to clients, whilst simultaneously putting the customer back in the core of the business.

This was a resounding success.

We are not a vendor to this company or just another consulting firm, we are a trusted partner, with skin in the game to deliver what was created on the joint mission as their change partner.

The client said,

"The fact I can hand pick a circle of experts on demand to really deliver something is why I went with this Teams as a Service model. It has given me the capability I need to make

this land and my permanent team are completely bought into it.

Change is hard enough, so you need a group of people who know what they are doing, have the independent mindset and are loyal to me, the organisation and not their sales target or the pyramid model.

It's quite simple – if I choose the A-Team, I expect the A-Team to stay to help me land what I need to land."

This was music to my ears, but let's explore why this model works.

Why were these projects so successful?

Well, first and foremost, all four companies understood the incessant need to be ahead of the curve in order to stay ahead of the curve.

As such, here is what characterised these four successful projects. There was:

- **Sponsorship** The times I've had 95% stick rate for hundreds of Interims is when I've had alignment and trust from the sponsor
- **Time for discovery and planning**
- **Time to cultivate teams** so the sponsors and I both treated it like a mission critical project
- **Alignment** (strategically between the board, HR, myself, the tight processes to create focus on delivering the outcome and those placed)
- **Embedded partnership** 100% trust and engagement - brought into the vision

So, let's explore those in a little more detail.

Sponsorship

At *Burberry*, we had all the sponsors, the VP and European IT Director in a room and we sat down together while they stress-tested our credentials, before spending time figuring out precisely what was needed.

At *Easynet*, I had already proved my mettle over time by iteratively placing some key roles that the *PSL* were struggling with.

As such, I began to gain trust.

However, a common denominator of success was the fact that there was a cohesive strategy, which included sponsors and HR, with the ultimate goal of getting some great broadband talent to *Easynet*. In fact, the consequence of placing such good talent was incredible, because they eventually caught the attention of *Sky*, who then bought the broadband part of their business out. A very pleasing impact.

Placing 250 Interims into that business with a 90% stick rate of success for anyone that I put in there is about as good as it gets. And it was cost effective, because they got everyone they needed when they needed them. As such, no time was wasted and the results speak for themselves. And the organisation was put under no unnecessary interview burden.

Time for discovery and planning

Allocating sufficient time for discovery and planning enables partners, such as myself, to get an all-important clear-brief. Such clarity empowered me to get into the mindset of each hiring manager.

Take *Burberry*.

We had thrashed everything out in the morning; we'd agreed a project plan, agreed briefs and I was able to really understand what, exactly, they were they looking for.

Not what would be on their job spec document, not what HR has produced that sat on a shared drive, but exactly what it was that our client was actually looking for? What types of personalities they like to be around? What gets the best out of them? How they critique a CV? And so on.

There is a key difference between allocating time for discovery and planning and allocating time to ping backwards and forwards to the market.

The latter is too frequently the status quo. I mean, how many times do you send out a brief, only for the agencies to come back to the line manager two weeks later who, by the way, is too busy to do anything, to say "Sorry, it's wrong. Back to market please."

A colossal waste of your time.

With *Burberry*, however, I was able to gather all the information I required from the outset; figure out exactly what each hiring manager was looking for, how that fitted into the grander strategic plan, and then build a process, which created accountability, urgency and had an end in sight.

The four-step process to top 5% talent was born. We'll dive into that in the next chapter.

With *Company X*, we spent time up front on the discovery session, mapping out the situation and formatting a transformation plan and recovery project, whilst also helping on the digital shift pilot opportunity.

Being able to deliver two separate teams for two separate missions with the same client and with urgency for that capability to be accelerated via our teams model in two weeks; that was only possible with time invested at the discovery phase.

Similarly, with *Company Y*, the *TaaS* model process worked with the CTO to discover the seeds of the transformation and create the vision/mission whilst naming the transformation.

This discovery phase was paramount to ensure the success of this hybrid consulting model.

Time to cultivate teams

With *Burberry,* thanks to time devoted to discovery and time provided for team-cultivation, we delivered. After gaining all that clarity, we went back to base, tapped into the network, went out to meet the individuals we were proposing to be a part of the project and delivered the team to the client.

With *Easynet,* I was given the time to go and hand-pick the very best people out there. It was not a *PSL* model of *we need these two* and four agencies go out, under duress, closing candidates within 10 seconds, because they do not want another *PSL* agency to sweet talk them. It did not involve the *PSL* standard of demanding emails to say I am representing you, creating agency wars.

I think people's reasons for allowing a wider *PSL* net to scan wider is defunct, quite simply because they do not. It feels like a race against time and, if you are on lower margins, you are not going to get the best recruiters. Conversely, with *Easynet,* I found the best five people and we delivered.

With *Company X*, we accepted the pressure involved with delivering in a short space of time, set the process and then casted the recovery team of five from our crowdsource network model.

We then presented the team, which was signed-off after a workshop, which was then pre-gelled and deployed in the space of two weeks for both missions.

The digital shift pilot was a team of three: *Digital Architect, Product Owner* and *Business Analyst*, all of whom worked with the executive to build and deliver on a pilot.

Because we had spent time on the discovery piece, we were able to make the most of the limited time we had to source the right team; we made every second of the team-sourcing process work.

Alignment (strategically between the board, HR, myself, the tight processes and those placed)

Meanwhile, with *Company Y*, we crowded the company with several Interims to create a business case within 40 days. This then became the pitch team, who delivered the business case, which was subsequently signed off and is now their number one business priority for the next three years.

Alignment between the board, HR, and our pitch team was vital to the success of this project.

Strategy, IT agenda and talent processes can become so mis-aligned, it's dangerous. And yet it is rare that I ever see the business, IT and people strategy aligned, let alone seeing the board, strategy, performance, administration and cultural behaviour aligned.

However, if you look at the more progressive companies that are pro-active to change and run by the younger generation, such alignment is more common place.

They know what good looks like. They pause, hack the process and align. They join the dots both internally and by creating their own alignment coalition, which will often include an accountability/alignment partner.

The result is that they rise towards *organisational credit*.

As a result of this focus on alignment, they come up with the right plan, they instill the right process and they find the right trusted partner who can deliver great people and teams to them who are aligned with all of this before they even start on the implementation.

Some might say that you need the right Trusted Partner at the front end, which is true, but if you get alignment, then you can get the right trusted partner in to help you with getting the right plan, and set up the right processes that are going to work for your organisation.

Once you've nailed that, you'll get the right people and the right teams. You just do.

Embedded partnership -
100% trust and engagement - brought into the vision

The resounding success of our work with *Company X* was only possible because the executive took the time out to work with us through the *4 Step Teams* model.

We had alignment, the process worked and we now have a trusted client and partner that will last a career.

Now we totally get the environment, so we are able to supply Top 5% resource into the organisation when they need bolstering or augmentation solutions within technology, change and digital.

Similarly, with *Company Y*, the transformation has been designed specifically with that organisation in mind and designed to incorporate exactly what will actually work for that specific organisation.

Not what has worked with other organisations, not what's going to be best for the management consulting firm and definitely not what iterative approach recruitment models gives you that waste so much time and lose business advantage.

Instead, we guided the transformation with the executive and with the senior leadership team – in partnership - coaching, transforming, directing and delivering with the company and their permanent staff and other partners.

We were embedded and brought into the vision.

Our main goal was to deliver it with them and leave them with a capability.

Our team of trusted Interim associates, led by our client engagement lead are the catalyst. It's about what is going to work for the customer after that team leaves. Being brought into the vision enables that.

The same can be said for *Easynet*.

Over time, I really got to know the whole board at *Easynet*, HR – two of the HRDs – and the HR advisers who were some of the best I have seen.

They were engaging with their line managers – and had a clear plan of how they could grow the business. They selected me as their third partner and gave me two-way access. I was embedded and we were all engaged. Consequently, I got to know the behaviours and what the counter culture would need to look like.

There was a major skills shortage but, because I was so loyal to what *Easynet* was doing, I was brought into the vision, brought into what the sponsors were looking to do. It was a race against time and I was up for it: totally motivated, on good terms, with a fantastic clarity of briefs, good system, which all led to the end result of great people, which led to the even better result of being bought out by *Sky*.

A huge success story.

This is what I love doing and it is one of the reasons I have moved away to set up on my own, because I have seen that way of engagement starting to slip as a result of big companies looking to commoditise the provision of people who have the capacity to have a huge impact in the organisation.

That questioning around whether organisations are really harnessing external talent to the levels that they can be, is what led me to figure out an alternative win-win model and launch forth with my own solution.

A solution that would see my team embedded in the board's business plan and creating value around the process.

I do not see many agencies that are embedded in board business plans and I do not see many agencies adding much more value, in fact, most are offering less and less value.

If you look at the value chain, lower margins screw down a supply to a single-figure mark up. And, on the other side, you see larger consultancy firms body shopping rather than managing a set of high deliverables that is created from a robust strategy to deliver upon. As a result, you cannot expect to get a hand-picked personalised service. If you want that, and you should; if you want a partner who can get you out of the problem and leave you with something sustainable for your business to operate on, you need to look elsewhere.

The business currency today is accuracy and speed. Saving the organisation by delivering people assets quickly and in volume every single time, that's what's needed.

More than ever, companies need partners who get technology, who get projects, who get that to find people that can mesh the two, understand business, understand technology, align both groups, and that is going to be a rare skill.

Because people are not a commodity.

My challenge to the market and to companies is to put your people agenda at the top of your priority list.

Don't outsource your recruitment of key knowledge workers.

And don't outsource your strategy to management consultancies.

Trusted Transformation

But how do you find the right trusted partner? One that will source and vet people according to your needs; a partner who has strong purposeful values and prioritises getting you quality talent over their own agenda? An agenda-less partner who is genuinely interested in helping your business to thrive?

The recruiters who have treated others as they wish to be treated; who have prioritised the provision of the best possible people over all other purposes; who have grown their networks into thriving communities filled with top quality candidates who are already working or looking to join the Interim revolution - those are the trusted partners to seek out (of which I am proud to say *Sullivan & Stanley* are one).

Unfortunately, currently, such trusted partners are few are far between. That said, they do exist and are worth devoting time to find.

Future recruiters need to treat their external experts like an internal consulting force harnessed for you; a resource to help you to get stuff done.

In order to source that consulting force, you need a partner who understands there is a different type of individual needed to enable your organisation to deliver on desired outcomes. You need teams of people who are agile, proactive, have a different breadth of skills, can take extreme ownership, and be a great positive influence on your wider business.

And you need a partner who can create a project team which delivers and then flows away when demand ebbs. This whole market is moving towards that ebbing and flowing.

So, what if companies could guarantee pre-packaged *A-Teams* who are ready to go; ready to make a difference?

Unfortunately, the perception is that consultancy firms can do that for you, but they have their own agenda and tend to be advisors rather than implementers.

And, more often than not, when they do provide teams, they are not the *A-Teams* that they hinted at during their initial meetings and they are often not perfectly aligned, because vetting takes time.

However, imagine if the vetting is second-to-none?

Imagine that the teams you get really are responsive *A-Teams* within a virtual consulting pool? Imagine if, alignment was placed firmly centre stage and you had access to an alignment workshop which enabled you to discover exactly what you need to align with the board, HR, your bigger picture strategy and processes?

You obviously need the right people at the front end, but you also need the right processes, and the model I have created will help you go from recognising who you need to hire to hiring in exactly the right help to deliver on your critical initiatives while boosting internal capability.

As such, the model that I am about to introduce to you can save a lot of pain, a lot of mistakes (which, at this speed of change are magnified) and add a lot of value.

By bringing in a transformative network and opening that up to my clients – they are able to dip in to the Interims on demand, the in-demand on-demand.

My service promise to any clients is that they will have access to top 5% Interim talent across many disciplines within leadership, advisory, agility, digital and technology trans-formation. So, whether it's to create alignment at scale, directly impact the performance of the business, recover poor change programmes or create the innovation agenda, we've got a team for that.

Teams as a Service provides Interim teams who have maximum impact wherever they are placed.

Teams as a Service is a genuinely viable alternative to consulting. It's lean consulting without the pyramid pressure, baggage or overheads that traditional consulting brings with it, with advice you can trust, as well as the delivery and implementation engine. And, as I said earlier, implementation is the key.

With *Teams as a Service*, there is structure added; a virtual consulting pool of elite independents with equal expertise (between 15-40 years of experience each) and no axe to grind, all working under an umbrella structure which enables great people to crowd around a problem and resolve it.

They can tell you which land mines to avoid and implement a strategy that has been fine-tuned amongst them, collaboratively, tapping into the immense power of an elite collective. Now we're talking.

When it comes to rising to the change challenge, *Teams as a Service* is as robust and elite a solution as you can get.

- No more mis-alignment
- No more body-shopping/CV sifting
- No more time-wasting/interview debt

As an Interim once said to me, *'Why would you pay £1,200 for a graduate to learn on the job, when you can pay £1,200 per day for me, and get 35 years worth of experience?'*

It's about optimising time (and money) by spending it doing the right things (discovering, planning and on-boarding).

We've got the on-site support. We do a lot of the on-boarding and the custodianship.

Teams as a Service is a form of crowdsourcing, only, the crowd has been sourced from an elite network of trustworthy agile talent, and the process is managed by a trusted partner who brings structure, experience and respect into a world that is commoditising people; a partner who values people as much as you do.

A high performing team trumps a cookie cutter methodology.

Key Takeaways

- Agility at scale enables a competitive advantage in a changing world. Simplicity is a key ingredient of agility.
- You can future proof your organisation and enable innovation by having an agile response to change, which taps into the collective minds of teams on tap. Such teams of *A-List* Interims can crowdsource around your problems. Multiple minds really are better than one.
- Interims deliver results, value for money and ROI; they are available immediately, come with a wealth of knowledge and expertise and are sufficiently objective, accountable and committed to getting results.
- The Hollywood model demonstrates how networks of independent and agile motivated talent can deliver supreme results to the archaic hierarchical studio system. Business across all industries is the same.
- Recruiters 2020 are network builders and connectors, curating talent pools to assemble top teams who deliver exceptional outcomes.
- Recruiters need to pivot away from the commodity race to use their skills in order to take on the management consulting firms.

Rapid Action Points

- Start thinking of Interims as an internal consulting force there to deliver value above and beyond.
- Some ideas to try instead of going to down the usual consulting or advisory route:
  - Appoint an Interim advisory council
  - Appoint an Interim board coach to advise and help with alignment

- Create ROI by signing up Interims on Statements of Works and Deliverables
- Start thinking of how you can bring in teams of Interims to help advise, coach, and upskill your permanent workforce to deliver outcomes and create a resident capability
- Look at Interims as a way to get diversity into board, leadership and workforce levels

- If you want to engage with the exec *Gig Economy*, maybe think of finding yourself a coach or mentor, start hanging around with NEDs, or perhaps take on a trusteeship.

- Bring in top 5% agile talent (ideally, *teams* of agile talent) to perform mission critical tasks and supplement permanent staff and boost capability. Take this for a test drive and see how it works out.

- Develop relationships with trusted partners in this space. How many trusted relationships have you really got with suppliers?

- Consider how these points will enable you reduce capability and speed gaps.

- Put top 5% talent and focused teams around projects at the top of your agenda. Ditch the commodity mindset.

Chapter 5

We've Got A Team For That –
The Four Pillar Teams as a Service Model

Chapter 5: We've Got A Team For That
The Four Pillar Teams as a Service Model (TaaS)

"If everyone had to think outside the box,
maybe it was the box that needed fixing"
Malcolm Gladwell, *Author and Speaker*

Great people are rare. Great teams are rarer. But it is now possible to source a stealth unit of great people – a *super team*, if you will.

Doing so has become my purpose over the past 15 years and is now my main driver in business: to spark an Interim revolution of the world's finest minds/experience and unite them to help solve business problems and execute trusted transformation.

As this book has demonstrated, given the ever-changing nature of the world of enterprise; aligning and planning effectively to source and retain the best people and knowledge possible is vital for optimal business performance.

Excellent recruitment is not a luxury. It has become a necessity to navigate the stormy seas we find ourselves in.

A good recruiter brings together opportunity, community and innovation. That's the future; getting people from where they are now to where they want to be by taking advantage of the changes that are happening, rather than burying our heads in the sand to avoid them, or carrying on as if nothing has changed.

Thankfully, having carried out significant research into what is and isn't working within the recruitment and consulting industry at large, I believe that this flexible solution for an emergent world does just what it needs to – it turns the *obstacle* of corporate talent drain that's flooding towards the gig/sharing/network/you economy into an opportunity that can be maximised by procuring cohesive teams of top quality Interims on-demand.

As such, it turns that obstacle into the best thing that could happen to your business.

It taps into the power of community and the collective mind to deliver results, manage change and transform corporate capability. Furthermore, given that consulting firm offerings are so frequently outdated, this never-done-before bespoke framework ticks the innovation box too.

Vitally, it puts the personal touch back into an industry that has been battered from one-size-fits-all models. And a personal service is what is so sorely needed today. We live in a relational world and I much prefer building career lasting relationships through a personalised service.

Remember my dad and his community? He also provided a *personal service*, which has always stuck with me. As his branch was based in Islington, he'd often give a pair of *Arsenal* tickets to his customers to bring them to the match. Back then, a home *Arsenal* game was even more of a great occasion than it is today.

My dad would make a judgment call on what to lend the businesses he worked with, based on the time he spent with the owner.

So off he'd go down Holloway Road, meeting with owners of furniture companies and pizzerias and the local kebab shop, chatting to builders and property developers and butchers. He'd always make the decision on the individual and their family situation, as much as their finances.

Notably, what he offered then was a personalised service. He didn't have the governance or regulation that banks have now, so he'd make a decision based on his expertise. And that personalised service is what industries have lost and so desperately need back.

Large organisations do not tend to choose that kind of personalised service. They're trying to outsource, give their resourcing to a *Preferred Supplier List (PSL)* or a consulting firm, but it's just not working.

I've always treated my suppliers like my clients over the years. I firmly believe, if businesses serving other businesses could just bring back some of that personalised service, there would be far more successful outcomes for businesses, large and small.

That enthusiasm to provide a personalised service by getting to know each individual I work with, both client and candidate side, that's part of my DNA.

Not only that, it's commercially sound. And here's why.

What my dad understood is that every business is different. And what's really working with the model I've been working on, is that every business is different.

As such, bespoke solutions to suit different companies and outcomes are what's required.

Not algorithms, not automation, not some new stunning piece of *AI* or robotic technology, which links individuals to companies, but a personalised service, which provides bespoke teams to suit precise needs of the board, executives and senior leaders.

Because there's too much at stake and there is too much human complexity involved to automate the process, or to provide the one-size-fits-all approach that is prevalent in today's recruitment and consulting marketplace.

That is why I have stepped boldly into the *trusted consultancy space* to start a movement, because people need to pause so they may look at what their company's problems are and get a solution that is bespoke to the company.

Because businesses and people and communities *still* matter.

And if we can blend a personal service with one which taps into the power of networks and communities too, that's a movement that can really move.

The Future of Recruitment and Virtual Consulting – The Rise of the Super Team

If Hollywood can do it in project squads to deliver great movies then surely there is a service around project squads to deliver change? Welcome to the challenger consulting model. It's lean, without pyramid pressure and without the overheads.

This model is called *Teams as a Service (TaaS)* and it enables you to future-proof your organisation via a new way of managing change.

Because, just as small is the new big, Interim teams are the new recruitment/consulting. Interspersing powerful teams of Interims will help you move iteratively into a better place, especially during a period of enterprise where no one knows what an emergent world is going to throw at you and where pivoting is a regularity.

It makes sense then that small iterations, small cycles, small teams are going to have the biggest impact.

Another notable gain from this model is knowledge-on-tap. After all, with all of this knowledge now available on demand as a direct consequence of the *Gig Economy* and shared/network economy, there's a dearth of intellectual capital, so why not tap into that? By providing *Teams as a Service*, there is now the possibility of solving all the recruitment, consulting, advisory and sourcing mistakes listed in *Chapter 3*.

By pausing to partner with a casting director who can provide rapid team formation to deliver a better outcome than you've ever experienced, you can win the war on talent and win the war on constant change while you're at it.

By putting a structure around this rising intellectual capital that's become available on-demand, you now have the opportunity to not only keep up but to stay and remain ahead, with a partner who can source great people you can really trust. As we've seen, today the business currency is *certainty, speed,* and *access to talent.*

So, that is what this framework strives to deliver.

With *TaaS*, we can deliver advisory on tap via our collective of top 5% recruiters, change agents and Interim leaders who crowd together to offer our clients on-demand trusted services around insight and advisory, around Interim consulting and trusted transformation.

Thanks to the network we've built, we can source brilliant change agents to make a real difference.

Clients can phone me to say, "Look, Pat, I've got an issue in this area, can you connect me with someone to help?" And I'll supply them with advisory on tap, rather than them having to pay an £80k-per-year subscription to an advisory firm.

As such, at *Sullivan & Stanley*, we are not just redefining recruitment, we are redefining the provision of advisory and trusted consulting through the crowd of the most experienced Interims around the globe.

We have curated into our *Change Society* community, who can be mobilised individually, or as teams.

Essentially then, *Teams as a Service* is an *A-Team Project Squad Curation Service* wrapped in a coaching and consultancy service.

Individuals and teams come from a crowdsourced model of trusted, hand-picked individuals matched to your needs to complement your lean internal team and help you deliver and succeed.

Having been in the business for 15 years, I've created such a good quality network of Interims that I am now in the fortunate position of being able to stitch and align teams together to deliver on the main change agenda, giving my clients the ability to flex on demand.

In our sales literature we talk about *re-aligning access from average people to wow people on demand*. But, as a reader of this book, I'm giving you a special ticket to learn a little more about how we do this.

So, what do you get with this new model for change?

How does *TaaS* enable you to be leaner and more responsive? How does *TaaS* enable you to get rapid results on demand?

Let's explore. Here's how ...

Deliver, Coach, Improve

TaaS provides us with the ability to deliver the following, every single time. Clients get:

- **Access to the in-demand, on-demand.**
  Access to a group of top 5% change agent leaders, when you want them, how you want them. In fact, with this model we can guarantee our clients the *A-Team* every time; an *A-Team* who can reduce complexity and redundancy within an organisation's technology estate, whilst coaching executives into the new world to deliver the future state.

- **Access to a range of capabilities including advisory, Interim and leadership bolstering, through to capability teams in agility, digital and technology transformation.**
  So, a number of transformation squads-for-hire within business and technology change, such as agile capsules, programme mobilisation/delivery/recovery and assurance teams, digital shift teams, innovation teams, target operating model teams and other technology capability teams.

- **A unique scientific vetting system and decision making process that marginalises the behaviour variable.**
  Essentially, all of our associates can facilitate future change and reduce complexity and have been tested rigorously before you see them.

- **The opportunity to figure out what you want and what you need as a result of a vigorous crowdsourcing discovery process** (which puts pay to making poor front end decisions that adversely affect the back-end. No more of that!) Especially with our *Workshop as a Service (WaaS)* product.

- **A pre-gelled team, a crowd-sourced co-operative of the best of the best.**
  Call them what you will: *change agents, problem-solvers* or *delivery stars* who I define as solution-focused, can-do, positive Interims, who come in, spin up and land, crowding around your problem or project and deliver the outcomes you need in order to manage change and thrive accordingly. We essentially hand-pick a high-performing group of people and pre-gel them together before entering your organisation. They can either enter as a *create new* solution or bolster your existing set-up and *cross pollinate* with your internal team.

- **A coaching and advisory arm to help with your internal capability and give you assurance and accountability for the short, medium and longer term.** You choose. This enables you to give your internal people a bit more responsibility as you bring in someone with a coaching record to help them. Otherwise, there is a good chance you are going to lose them. Retention of good people is as vital as recruitment of them.

- **The personal touch.** *TaaS* is essentially virtual consulting with a very lean umbrella at the top, so the client engagement lead actually takes ownership of the project and has custodianship. We want it to work as much as you do, and so it does.

- **Value.**
  The model aims to go the extra mile to ensure that you get an impressive ROI and are left with a sustainable change capability.

We'll explore how the model adds value and obliterates the mistakes that traditional current recruitment and consulting consistently makes later in the chapter. For now, allow me to explain the model in a little more detail.

The *4-Step TaaS model* that helps companies access the top 5% of external expert talent is as follows:

- Discover
- Create
- Mobilise
- Sustain

This framework allows a trusted partner to come in and help you to pause, get alignment, set up process and deliver results.

So, let's take a look at each of these.

Discover - Hit The Pause Button To Get Alignment, Cohesion and Solution Clarity

As we've seen, the costs and consequences of messing projects up are huge. Profits plummet. People leave. Heads roll. So why don't we just stop?

Why don't we just hit the pause button and set up a diagnostic base, bring in a casting director, an agility coach, an organisational design therapist and a change 'hand-holder' and have a workshop to get everything nailed at the front end, so that we may avoid back end problems down the line?

The value of doing so is cohesion and focus and a clear mission to be executed on. The outcome is alignment and success.

Investing time at the beginning to get unification and clarification is incredibly worthwhile to avoid the common mistakes made in recruitment and consulting today.

Pausing allows you the space to get proactive rather than reactive.

It also enables an assessment of alignment so that we can ensure that the vision/mission/purpose of the business is aligned with people, both on the ground and in the board room, and that everything and everyone is aligned with the culture, the processes and even the administration.

This is vital as there is often cultural and behavioural misalignment in recruitment process and delivery.

Once we've discovered the key 'alignment pillars' we can then hold everyone involved accountable to that alignment.

We look at ways to do that, including methods of communicating transformation to the wider business, be it via a monthly all-staff webinar, *a la Google*, or other means (which we can help develop using our transformation communications capability).

When you've been in the recruitment business as long as I have, you know that, when you get stakeholders around the table and listen to them properly, you get a feel for them as individuals and intuitively know what type of personalities are going to gel. You are able to drill down to the specific outcomes they want to achieve and establish a process and plan to get the right people for them who'll deliver stunning results.

That is what this discovery piece is all about. It's pointless planning a recruitment or consulting solution or package without it.

In order to know what *good* will look like in 12-months time and tune in to the key behaviours and capabilities needed for success, a facilitated *corporate pause workshop* is a no-brainer.

It helps you to pause, align and discover the best route forward and establish what talent is required to help get you there. This gives your trusted partner clarity around culture, *vision, mission* and *purpose*.

It also enables *IT/Business/People alignment* and a *capability assessment* to establish where the gap is within leadership, delivery and mentality.

This knowledge enables your partner, such as *Sullivan & Stanley,* to work out a clear one, two, three month talent sprint and define required results in a clear accountability agreement, so everyone knows who is responsible for what and why so.

The outcome of this discovery piece is a proposed solution that focuses on either creating a new team or bolstering/replacing an existing one.

The result is *holistic alignment* and *organisational credit*. Oh, and of course, clarity, direction and the benefits that come with winning the war on talent.

During our discovery phase we can carry out a full

capability gap assessment, figure out precisely where the pain points are, define a solution and agree an outcome that will close that capability gap. Later on, we work with our clients to ensure that the gap remains closed.

It could be that an agility capsule is required? Or maybe you have a failing programme and need a hit squad?

There might be weak leadership and the requirement for a CIO or CTO to hand hold or for a coach to hold up a mirror to those leaders and coach them?

Perhaps your programme is going reasonably well, but you could do with an elite project manager and killer organisational architect to come in with augmentation capsule?

Maybe you've got quite a good permanent team, but they're immature. Maybe they've never seen a transformation of this size, so you'd like some sort of coaching element?

Or perhaps you think you're doing the right things but need some assurance over what you're doing and provision of a heat map that flags up what's good and what needs tweaking strategy-wise. Maybe you're just not getting projects out quick enough and want to get products out to market in 30 days instead of 90 days?

Whatever team you need, they are within the network I have built over 15 years in the business, resourcing over 100 successful transformations.

In addition, the power of the *Change Society's* network and thousands of years of collective experience successfully delivering transformation is accessible to the business world.

We have a team for that, for any problem being thrown at you. We figure out what is the team going to look like?

Whether we need to build around a leader or carefully select equal experts into our teams, we've got a team for that and, once we've discovered your precise needs, we can move on to step two and create a bespoke aligned and vetted pre-gelled hit squad from our crowdsourced network.

Create a Bespoke, Aligned and Vetted Hit Squad

After spending time with our clients during the discovery phase, we go away and build a team based on the clear brief we've all invested time in.

The value is supreme vetting.

We match mission and needs with a team using our unique vetting funnel to guarantee the outcome - the best team possible. Our structured team-gelling exercise enables us to create a high-impact, high-valued, well-structured team.

That aligned, pre-gelled and structured team hasn't existed until now, and that is the value that I am passionate about bringing to the market via *Sullivan & Stanley* and via this book.

Because, as more and more people read this book and demand change within the recruitment and consultancy market, by seeking out trusted partners who can provide this kind of service, the *Interim Teams Revolution* will flourish and create a global mutual win-win-win – a market where the client wins, the Interim team member (candidate) wins and the *TaaS* provider wins, hence disrupting the status quo in today's models, which is my personal mission.

A change for the client, a change for the candidate and evolution of this industry.

Having picked the brains of the client during our *Discovery phase,* we've got the vision, mission, purpose and clarity; we've done the cultural assessment and capability review.

The service and solution definition has been done and the client has committed.

During our *Create phase*, we've crowdsourced from our network and carried out the cultural vetting and alignment which leads us to the bespoke team selection where goals and strategy are aligned and we pre-gel the team.

Within our network, by creating a pipeline of worthwhile opportunities, we are attracting the best of the best. This means we can provide a personalised service of a hand-picked team for our clients.

Every executive is different. Every company is different, hence why I feel strongly that bespoke solutions have a greater chance of successful delivery in organisations; so working with you not for you.

And our early adopters of the *TaaS* approach are agreeing wholeheartedly.

Opportunity + community
= top 5% team creation and rapid results on demand.

Creating rapid results on demand by creating top teams is the sweet spot of this structured virtual consulting pool. Once the team has been approved, it's time to mobilise and on-board that team.

Mobilise - Fast Start To Make Shift Happen

The mobilisation part of the process is where we prepare to make *shift happen*. We empower the teams with a fast start, provide the tooling and carry out the on-boarding. This is where we go into more detail with our teams to explore the *Do's and Don'ts* of the culture, book meetings with the key dependencies and provide support via on-site coaching/mentoring support and custodianship.

We align the internal and external partners to optimise the knowledge/skill share/transfer.

We set up accountability and alignment sessions, work through a few problems and scenarios, create delivery predictability and ensure our coaching wrapper is in place. The outcome is a fast-tracked mission-ready team; the value is impact – with a pre-gelled on-boarded tooled-up team, execution of the mission begins, and is therefore achieved, sooner.

The client has the option to be part of this mobilisation process and be part of on-boarding or not, because we stitch the team together and arrive on site with that fully pre-gelled team and mobilise that team; we get them working immediately and kickstart them into action from day one. They hit the ground running in a fast start scenario and this saves so much time. Fundamentally, the time spent upfront gaining clarity and understanding proves its worth during this mobilisation phase, because the team are ready (and raring) to go.

Sustain – Support, Enhance and Upskill Internal Capability

Once *TaaS* has built, supported, enhanced and upskilled your internal capability, organisational credit continues.

Importantly, the Interim *Teams* model, underpinned by coaching is vital because it transforms your business; improves your organisational health; and delivers a capability that is sustainable after exiting.

As illustrated below, coaching is a vital part of the process within our *Interim Coaching Concept*. Working with *Company Y (*see p171), we coached and aligned the board and leadership team, and upskilled the workforce transforming them to a faster-delivery, product-centric organisation.

The Interim Coaching Concept

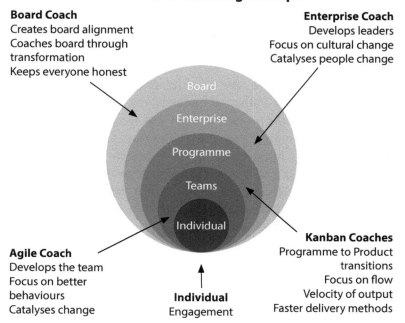

Board Coach
Creates board alignment
Coaches board through
transformation
Keeps everyone honest

Enterprise Coach
Develops leaders
Focus on cultural change
Catalyses people change

Agile Coach
Develops the team
Focus on better
behaviours
Catalyses change

Individual
Engagement

Kanban Coaches
Programme to Product
transitions
Focus on flow
Velocity of output
Faster delivery methods

We then continue to coach and mentor permanent people through a variety of methods to help sustain the value that was delivered through the team. As such, the outcome is that you have capability after we've left. So the value is sustainability and a workforce with low attrition and high engagement.

The *TaaS* ongoing agility and alignment coaching wrapper is available via subscription to dip in and out of. This means, as well as ensuring that the team pass on their knowledge whilst working in the business, existing staff continue to benefit long after the *TaaS* team has moved on to their next project to ensure sustainability.

We're looking to knowledge share and upskill, in order to maintain and sustain the value, which is why we run alignment accountability sessions with an ongoing coaching record to assist our clients internally, after the team has left the building. In this way, if programmes slip back from green into amber on the heat map, we can get people back in for a few days or coach existing staff to sustain positive outcomes via a consistently proactive solution.

So there you have it. A different way of recruitment and consulting that I hope will become an *Interim Teams Revolution*.

The status quo of Interims and regular recruitment is comparatively unstructured.

As I've illustrated over the previous pages, it's a lottery and, crucially, it has to be managed by the client.

With *TaaS*, we ensure that we get the most from the team we supply you with. From the clarity around the brief, the parameters and timescales, to the regular accountability reviews, coaching, and transfer of knowledge at the end of the assignment; by putting a structure in place, we can help clients move from A to B and help them to stay where they need to be and continue to grow accordingly.

How TaaS Prevents The Current 7 Recruitment and Consulting Mistakes

"Trust is like an eraser; it gets smaller and smaller with every mistake."
Jay Shetty, *Vlogger, presenter and former monk*

In business, as service providers, the fewer mistakes we make, the more able we are to build trust. And, if this process has taught me anything, it's that a trusted hybrid recruitment and consulting partner offering a hybrid model is an absolute must and yet so sorely lacking in today's business world.

So, if the future of work and recruitment involves hiring teams of Interims, how do we ensure that we don't repeat the mistakes we've made in the past? How do we create certainty in this uncertain world?

For me, it all boils down to agility and alignment. Seamlessly delivering those generates trust.

To illustrate, let's revisit those seven key recruitment mistakes that we explored in *Chapter 3* to see how *TaaS* literally obliterates them.

1. Reactive Recruitment Caused By Poor Planning and Lack of Alignment

The *Discovery* phase of the *TaaS* model provides the client and the partner with a chance to plan effectively and align accordingly. It's crucial to pause long enough to figure out who is needed, why so, what they will need to do and how that aligns with strategy around where the business is now and where it aims to be.

Furthermore, the *Discovery* and *Sustain* phases of the model enable a move away from a reactive mode of planning and lack of alignment working to a proactive mode, especially with coaching and independent facilitation.

2. Companies Interview Far Too Many Candidates To Get The Talent

What if, instead of hiring under duress as a result of the time-consuming nature of recruitment where companies interview far too many candidates, you were able to hire with confidence instead?

If you have the right trusted partner in place; one who takes the time themselves to get to know your business needs and acts swiftly to pull in the right people - all of them excellent and aligned – you instantly up your game. You get rid of the over-interviewing issue because you don't need to do the interviewing.

With *TaaS,* poor vetting is replaced by a solid vetting process with no more gambling on outcomes. There is no more outsourcing your recruitment, no more *PSL* lottery, or giving ownership of your strategy to management consulting firms.

Those tired methods are mistakes you should avoid.

Let's be honest here, interviews are a blunt instrument. Everyone can play the *capability game* and make themselves sound better than they really are in practice.

Workshops provide an environment that enables truth.

For a start, workshops are less formal and more interactive

than traditional interviews; they enable delivery partners to better understand how candidates approach problems and uncover what their personalities are like in real-time.

You quickly see a more comfortable and therefore better version of a candidate when they feel more relaxed and better able to demonstrate their strengths. The result is a more authentic and accurate presentation and perception of candidates.

What's more, with *TaaS* you literally tap into a knowledge worker vetting funnel which sources the best available change agents on-demand. The network that the teams are part of enables us, as trusted partners, to get to know each candidate really well.

This further allows us to source the best of the best quickly. Because we've taken time to pause upfront, we have a better understanding of the precise requirements and can match and align the capabilities and behaviours to the culture and strategy. Hard and soft skills are clarified. Behaviours, values, mindset are all understood long before the vetting process. As a consequence, mis-hiring is minimalised. In fact, it just doesn't tend to happen with the *TaaS* model.

TaaS also streamlines the recruitment process by leaping over the hurdles of bureaucracy. The framework and process is lean and agile, just like the talent it curates. This saves time that is traditionally spent by HR, leaders and procurement getting involved in the recruitment process.

Less cooks result in a supreme rather than spoiled broth.

With *Company Y* (see p171) we have got the ratio down to one introduction via a workshop to one associate placement via our rate card managed service. So zero interview debt. Historically, their *PSL* stats were 30 CVs to eight interviews for no result.

3. Obsession With Cost

Prioritising money-saving over quality-hiring is, as we've seen, a false economy. *TaaS* is not a cheap option so it does not create back-end problems that poor front-end decisions generate. When you choose a trusted partner who delivers prime people, you get more bang for your buck.

Still not convinced? Re-read *Chapter 5* on how Interims and teams provide more value and return on investment than you might think. Hiring well is valuable.

And, if you hire right first time, you will ironically end up saving money that you would have had to spend rectifying the problems created by *PSLs* and traditional body-shopping. *TaaS* is also not as expensive as management consultancies but it's high value for a fair cost.

4. Hiring a Recruitment Process Outsourcer (RPO)

Outsourcing the ownership of your recruitment entirely is not worth the risk. Far better to work *with* a trusted partner, which is how *TaaS* works. We work with you to find people who can positively influence your business, even after they have left, so there is no misjudging of IT/change capabilities needed in the first instance and no gamble on who you end up with. Always hire an expert capability partner for IT and change.

5. Busting The Preferred Supplier Myth (PSL)

Recruitment requires flexibility, which *Preferred Suppliers* with uniform arrangements fail to offer.

Different issues, problems, requirements, projects each need different solutions from a more-than-one-size model i.e., a model that takes the need for flexibility into consideration and matches the right people to suit the specific needs at any given time. *TaaS* is flexible because of the constant communication and the responsive nature of the service.

TaaS is therefore good for corporate health, morale and competitive advantage because it delivers flexibly based the needs it uncovers during the discovery process. *TaaS* provides certainty, because it responds to needs rather than reacting to situations; the opposite of how traditional *PSL* models work. It gets rid of poorly vetted CVs being sent over by agencies from the same pool of mediocre talent.

The networks contain the best of the best Interim talent to help people get some real game changers into their operation. And the rigorous vetting, pre-gelling and onboarding processes de-risks the process completely, as does the initial discovery period.

A trusted partner will know what you want and then provide it. With the right model, one that focuses as much on alignment as it does agility, it's as simple as that.

Furthermore, because *TaaS* enables candidates to work on projects they enjoy and have the perfect mix of skills, knowledge and personalities to suit, they trust the partner as much as the client creating a web of trust and goodwill amongst the best talent out there and the best companies to work for.

6. Entering The Recruitment Lottery In The First Place

You will tend to find that people sourced from a trusted partner's network won't be the kind of people who have their CV on databases or apply for adverts. They do not need to, because they are the kind of people who get referrals, such is their level of competency and specialism.

As such, *TaaS* gives you access to a talent pool which has the kind of talent you need and deserve within it – i.e., good quality hires every single time. Evidently, with *TaaS* there is no need to gamble on outcomes any more.

Rather, there is an opportunity to recruit the best individuals who can deliver outcomes and exceed rather than fail to meet expectations. Fundamentally, it serves nobody to continue along the road of uncertainty. *TaaS* brings certainty to the recruitment and consulting space, to partner with you and take away the pain of older models.

7. Falling Into The Expensive Consultancy Pyramid Trap

When you realise that you get what you pay for when it comes to recruitment it's important to also realise that, if you are going to spend a little more on sourcing the right people for the right situation, you need to be able to fully trust that they have *your* best interests at heart, rather than their own.

While this is, sadly, not always the case when you join the expensive consultancy pyramid trap, you can rest assured that a *TaaS* partner does what they do to serve you. That's a priority.

That's why you'll always get the *A-Team* working *with* you who will source an *A-Team for you.* How do you know that for sure?

Because *TaaS* originated from a space of service, from a purpose and mission of genuinely wanting to improve the recruitment and consulting market by giving those who are paying recruiters a better way of sourcing the right people at the right time; by giving those in their network the best opportunities to suit their skills and by enabling companies to close the capability and speed gap and flourish in business.

Because, until now, no-one has been truly partnering with an organisation to help them embrace today's aggressive digital disruption. The consequence of this purpose-driven service is that *TaaS* providers will thrive too.

Creating a better way of doing things that gets companies and candidates the results they deserve drives true value.

Indeed, that's why alignment is such a high priority for us as creators of the *TaaS* model. Alignment bolsters ability and agility.

Getting into the behaviours and cultural alignment between the candidate and company is vital to optimise gains for both client and candidate, yet it is often alignment that consultancies fall down on, according to the interviews I've conducted. Ultimately, if you are paying a premium, you deserve a service that is jam-packed with value, a service that is responsive, a service that provides alignment with key dependencies, just as *TaaS* does.

A Better Way

As these seven mistakes prove, what is needed is something you haven't seen before.

A new, more agile, responsive and smart way of recruiting top talent for those who are really serious about closing their capability and speed gaps so that companies, the city, investors, company boards and shareholders can readily align their paradigms to pivot into the new world.

We've reached the limit using traditional operating models and management hierarchies. And yet *flatter* alternatives don't provide the structure needed to harness the power of a collaborative, aligned and lean workplace.

Interim consulting does.

It provides something different that doesn't create Armageddon by turning the operating structure on its head. Instead it offers us a way to flexibly navigate the more complex scenarios whilst gaining competitive advantage too.

Let's be honest. We don't know exactly what the future will hold, none of us do, except that change will be driving it. Frankly, we don't know which industry is going to get *Ubered* next.

We do know that the only constant nowadays is change as the business world is transformed continually by the on-demand economy.

We also know that organisations and executives and decision makers are struggling to find partners they can trust to mobilise a volume of talent quickly to deliver outcomes. We know there is a spectrum between what a *PSL* and *RPO* can offer, what a reputable agency can offer and what a consultancy can offer and that, even at the higher value end of this spectrum, there are problems.

It makes sense to choose a trusted partner who can source top 5% Interim teams who come in and partner with your permanent people to rapidly close the capability gap and deliver game-changing outcomes.

I left the comfort of the larger agency world to set up *TaaS* and a *challenger brand* with *Sullivan & Stanley* - a remarkably different proposition to help companies deal with this emergent change - a different type of service for a very different world; a collective of transformers whose aim is to keep clients out of the problem, improve capability and provide the much-needed business agility to embrace ever changing market conditions.

And I know I've done the right thing, because change is continual and this solution helps companies to manage it.

In this day and age of uncertainty and continual change, why wouldn't you try this model out?

Perhaps, you're thinking it's not going to work with the executives?

Funnily enough, we have a solution for that.

Our agile capsule is being used by some *FTSEs* at the moment where small teams of between three and six have been given a small project to iteratively deliver.

The hard benefits have been reported and celebrated at executive level which results in support for further transformation.

TaaS removes uncertainty with value-added assurance around delivery by mixing the top 5% recruiters with SME industry experts to bring a combination of *on-demand* services to organisations facing 21st century transformation.

Key Takeaways

- Accurate recruitment of top 5% is not a luxury. It's a necessity in today's disruptive world.
- Great people are rare. Great teams are rarer. But super teams and knowledge on tap are now accessible via *TaaS*.
- A good recruiter/delivery partner brings opportunity, community and innovation.
- *TaaS* is a lean challenger model of virtual consulting which provides project squads to deliver change and other mission-critical outcomes.
- Agile mindsets within small teams are the future. The benefits of small cross-functional teams are that communications flow easily within a trusted team environment and individuals are more engaged in their work.
- You're only a week away from correcting a mistake with top agile teams.

Rapid Action Points

- Create time to handpick the best people for the mission, the outcome and the opportunity.
- Start incorporating the Interim coaching concept in your organisation from the board down to the team through to the individual.
- Choose a part of your current project portfolio and create a cross-functional team consisting of business and technology to help with alignment.
- Consider which of these are most valuable to you:
  - Time to discover and respond to needs
  - Access to an in-demand wide range of capability on demand
  - Coaching

- Upskilling of internal capabilities
- Choose a part of your project portfolio and implement a *TaaS* approach in a parallel universe model away from the traditional organisational structure i.e., start up mentality without the bureaucracy.
- Try teams crowded around a purposeful mission.

Conclusion:

A Vision For The Future

Conclusion: A Vision For The Future

"The mind, once stretched by a new idea,
never returns to its original dimensions."
Ralph Waldorf Emerson, *American Poet*

The Vision

Disruption is here and more is coming.

Organisations and Executives need to tackle unprecedented change and uncertainty to remain competitive and, frankly, to stay in a job.

But change is hard.

And it's getting harder and more complex.

Sadly, as we've explored throughout this book, past practices are failing to deliver.

It's time for something new.

It's time to change the way you recruit and execute.

It's time to embrace the power of decent trusted head-hunters who can curate top talent from a network and generate the opportunity and untapped potential of wisdom on demand.

I've seen the frustration on the faces of both clients and candidates alike.

I've seen the company waste that has accrued by mis-hiring, when I've been in to pick up the pieces and I don't want that for you. I don't want that for organisations which deserve to thrive.

My vision through this new model and challenger business is:

- Future proof organisations and their operating models.
- Help my clients solve organisational and technical debt.
- Guide older established companies to morph into more responsive ones to avoid disruption.
- Ignite change and innovation in industry and help people where they need it most.
- Connect high performing Interims and teams of high performing Interims to organisations looking to change.
- Help people deliver key projects and solve business problems in an agile way.
- Bring the Hollywood teams effect to Interim management.
- Help CXO executives own the Innovation Agenda and thrive at board level.
- Be right in the heart of this booming *Knowledge* and *Executive Gig Economy*.
- Change the way the world engages with Interim professionals, help them stand out and find their voice through our *Change Society* community.

Because I believe that Interim responsive teams are the future for delivering change in a manageable way where everybody wins.

This book has shown how teams of high end Interims can make a big difference, and offers a model for engaging such teams to drive rapid and lasting change.

We've also flagged up and highlighted the range of problems and mistakes companies want to avoid.

The *TaaS* framework has been developed to ensure that you never again need repeat those mistakes or get stuck when you encounter those problems.

Because, that is what enterprise and entrepreneurship are all about: creating fresh solutions to solve problems whilst creating value. Innovation is about offering something better than the status quo. That's the place that *Sullivan & Stanley* came from, with the belief that the most valuable work done in this changing business landscape is done by teams of people who work well together. And that's why the Interim *crowdsourcing TaaS* model was born.

Of course, what is innovative one day soon becomes the norm. And I hope that this will be the case for the *Interim Revolution* – to move from a place of revolution and disruption of the existing status quo, towards a place of evolution where it may become a new and better, status quo.

The change I want to see in the world is for:

- Every company to have access to the flexible workforce they need, to cope with emergent change and benefit their organisation.
- A structured Interim team revolution to become the genuine alternative to consulting firms i.e., a new hybrid model – taking the best of recruitment and consultancy and the Interim talent pool to solve business and talent problems and create business agility and trusted transformation.
- Businesses to stop making poor front end decisions.
- Enterprises to have the agility they need to thrive in a globalised market.
- To spark an *Interim Revolution* of the globes finest Interim professionals to solve business problems.
- Help the individual genuinely achieve a work/life balance satisfaction and help inspire the future of work.
- *Sullivan & Stanley – The Change Society*, to be the *hub of opportunity* for Interim professionals by 2020 and *the world's first change partner*, powered by the *Interim crowd*.

We've seen how the solution I've put forward in this book solves the mistakes that the current modus operandi of recruitment and consulting perpetuates.

Now we need people, forward-thinking, community-minded people like you to get out into the world and use this model, talk about it, share it, write about it, spread it and create a growing market for it.

If you would like to discover more about the *TaaS* model I invite you to experience the immediate positive impact of a *Discovery* session. You can reach me via:

TIR@ sullivanstanley.com
www.sullivanstanley.com

In fact, as a community of executives, recruiters and Interims, we've got a responsibility here to help organisations make it.

It's almost like a duty of care to help sustain enterprise during an era where training budgets are disappearing, organisations are struggling, their revenues are on the decline.

We need to collectively stop, pause and tackle change effectively, together. The catalysts for positive change are already in place. And the *Gig Economy* is growing rapidly.

We know that the *Gig Economy* is already providing knowledge workers, accomplished professionals, consultants and executives with the kind of control over their career and work-life integration/satisfaction that they've never yet experienced. And this business will support any executives, change agents, Interims in their gig career.

We know that retirement is being rewritten because of this shift towards work-life balance that this *Gig Economy* provides, and we know that companies are taking advantage of this ability to engage in a nimble way with a highly skilled global talent pool, and, in doing so manage costs more effectively, leverage specialist skills and thrive.

My own experience of what is wrong with the recruitment and consulting industry and what is right with it, combined with the direct experience of hundreds of others and the research I've undertaken has created a perfect storm for me to figure out this solution – this hybrid virtual global change partner powered by the Interim crowd.

Most established organisations have three major problems. They don't have the people to change *(Capability Gap)*. They don't have the agility to change, *(Speed Gap - Org and Tech Debt)* and they are sitting in operating models that were fit decades ago, but not today. And their current routes to capability are failing.

Technology is changing the game.

Newer, faster, more responsive, disruptive businesses are taking their market share.

It is now a business imperative for an organisation to have their own change capability, but most are under-prepared.

Enter the *Interim Revolution*.

It all comes back to my childhood experience of how people make the difference in business; how I watched my father rise from licking stamps to become divisional CEO for a global bank, and how I witnessed what made the difference and cultivated his success was the fact that he always surrounded himself with great people.

Furthermore, once he found them, he got to know them and he looked after them.

Nurturing connections is something I've inherited with immense gratitude from him.

And it is this that has enabled me to create a trusted network. It is this that has enabled me to uncover what people really want and need and provide it to them, to enable people to achieve the outcomes they desire by placing the people they require; people they can trust and teams of people they can trust.

I'm an opportunity maker, I connect people; it's what I love doing as a change agent. I've helped many organisations to design transformation teams that deliver.

And yet, the model that has served me well for 15 years is being broken up into little bits. Being the change is the only way I could use my understanding around the problems that technical, organisational and people debt are creating.

Interim teams are the future because, as I've discovered, people want to crowd round a mission; deliver, disperse and move on to the next project.

Hence why organising the world's first network of change agents through our *Change Society* community has become my mission and being a positive force in the evolution of global business and giving people and companies access to freedom and opportunity, has become my purpose.

I believe that my dream: to spark an Interim revolution using my new model for the flexible knowledge economy as the touch-paper, has begun.

The *TaaS* model is where my journey has led me to – that's why I have created this model to spark an *Interim Revolution* and to create, fuel and sustain this booming *Executive/Knowledge Gig Economy*. I hope you will join me.

There's important work to be done in the world and there are important companies of all sizes out there doing it, or trying to. But, with the best will in the world, they can only achieve their mission and purpose if they have an agile and capable team. One that can adapt quickly enough to get this important work done. I want to help companies to meet this challenge – to become agile and aligned – instead of using outdated models of working and recruiting that are no longer serving them.

After all, it is enterprise that shapes our future, and those enterprises need people who are capable of doing their best work. Because people matter, especially when it comes to managing change and other complex challenges.

Such challenges require close collaboration among teams with a range of high-quality skills and diverse specialisms. Command-and-control is the Achilles heel; flexible agile teams are the way forward.

With *Sullivan & Stanley* I'm creating a company that has access to the top 5% of people. We've got a propriety client engagement and teams model for rapid assembly, management and deployment of teams. All we need now is for forward-thinking companies to trial this once. Those who do are amazed.

The Manifesto

My manifesto for those serious about closing the capability and speed gaps is as follows:

- **Small is the new large.** Change can be efficient with small iterations and focused teams.
- **Outcome based teams is the future of resourcing and consulting.**
- **Teams are the new recruitment and consulting; the old recruitment model is dying.** A collection of minds crowding round a problem, co-managed, is more effective than single individuals being fired into your department to be managed.
- **Business agility is a necessity not a luxury**, so harness agile Interim talent in order to become flexible and agile at the teams level *and* throughout the business.

To recap, these are the next steps you need to take in order to tackle change and remain competitive.

- **Surround yourself with great people, because it is people who make the difference.** And now you have access to advisory and change teams on tap.
- **Pause often and invest time.** In doing so, you will avoid many of the mistakes and poor front end decisions that are being made and repeated in the recruitment space today. Pausing enables you and your hybrid recruitment/ consulting partner to get forensic from day one

and gain clarity on the nitty-gritty of what you need. People often like to start by engaging us with a workshop, where we discover what is needed to generate the best results.

- **Get aligned.** From the board to the boots on the ground, from the processes in place to the people and partners you work with; from the culture of your organisation to the behaviours of your Interims – alignment enables a smoother journey.
- **Make trust a priority.** Trust is efficient and, with a trusted partner, the world is your oyster.

An Invitation

So, if you want to run a workshop around some of your problems and discuss ideas around solutions, contact me at:

TIR@sullivanstanley.com

www.sullivanstanley.com

Our capsule team could be put to work in your organisation within days of reading this book. (That's essentially a micro version of the *TaaS* model on one project of work).

We are starting something here; we're creating a movement. It's moving forward and we're inviting you to come and talk to us.

We have been designed to help the individual and their Interim journey, whilst also helping the enterprise to try something different; a fresh approach with some new connections.

Because, as my dad always said:

"People matter in business and surrounding yourself with the best people makes all the difference."

References

Books

- Van den Born. A. (2013) *The Fuzzy Firm – The new networked organisation in the Gig Economy*. Born to Grow.
- Little. J. (2014). *Lean Change Management – Innovative Practices for Managing Organisational Change*. HMExpress.
- McChrystal. Gen. S. (2015). *Team of Teams : New rules of engagement for a complex world*. Penguin.
- Priestley. D. (2014). *Key Person of Influence*. ReThink Press.
- Younger. J. & Smallwood. N. (2016). *Agile Talent – How to source and manage outside experts*. Harvard Business Review Press.

Articles

- http://www.forefrontmag.com/2015/06/on-demand-executives-your-secret-weapon/
- http://content.time.com/time/magazine/article/Blockbuster
- http://www.cio.com/article/2985406/leadership-management/crowdsource-your-way-to-a-better-it-team.html
- http://crowdsourcingweek.com/what-is-crowdsourcing/
- https://appirio.com/wp-content/uploads/2016/05/ITTalentWarsandtheGigEconomyReport.pdf
- http://www.cio.com/article/2985406/leadership-management/crowdsource-your-way-to-a-better-it-team.html
- http://www.cio.com/article/3083800/cio-perspectives/who-s-the-digital-transformation-boss-and-why-should-it-be-the-cio.html
- businessagilityworkshop.com
- http://www.cio.com/article/3086048/hiring/it-talent-biggest-roadblock-to-digital-transformation.html
- https://twitter.com/paul_framp/status/
- http://www.telegraph.co.uk/culture/film/film-blog/9806615/

Blockbuster-no-tears-for-the-film-rental-giants-demise.html
- https://www2.deloitte.com/content/dam/Deloitte/global/ Documents/HumanCapital/gx-dup-global-human-capital-trends-2016.pdfhttp://www.forbes.com/sites/gregsatell/2015/09/05/ we-dont-need-the-best-people-we-need-the-best-teams/
- http://www.responsive.org/manifesto/
- http://aug.co/responsive-enterprise-transformation/#home
- http://www.agilecio.net/
- https://medium.com/the-ready/six-leadership-principles-for-competing-in-the-modern-era
- http://raconteur.net/business/on-demand-freelance-workers-are-on-the-rise
- http://www.forbes.com/sites/gregsatell/2015/09/05/we-dont-need-the-best-people-we-need-the-best-teams/
- https://centricdigital.com/blog/digital-trends/TaaS-is-the-new-hr-mode
- http://www.forbes.com/sites/gregsatell/2015/09/05/we-dont-need-the-best-people-we-need-the-best-teams/
- http://www.holacracy.org/implement
- http://www.forbes.com/sites/kaytiezimmerman/2016/07/12/ how-crowdsourcing-is-transforming-the-workplace/#14cb3c4d5e73
- http://www.fastcompany.com/3057210/the-future-of-work/why-the-future-of-work-will-look-a-lot-like-hollywood
- https://www.quora.com/Will-Silicon-Valley-one-day-create-talent-agencies-like-Hollywood-that-will-own-engineering-talent-and-help-engineers-cut-deals-and-find-projects
- http://www.bain.com/story/firm-of-future/
- https://hbr.org/2017/07/how-to-make-agile-work-for-the-C-Suite
- https://hbr.org/2016/06/to-seize-the-future-create-a-leadership-circle
- https://www.bcgperspectives.com/content/articles/transformation-large-scale-change-people-organization-building-capabilities-transformation-that-lasts/

Acknowledgments

Big thanks to all my associates in *The Change Society* and executive clients who continue to support this journey I'm on.

And especially to my advisors Christian McMahon, Thomas Power and Andrew Priestley for all their guidance and mentoring.

The first year of *Sullivan & Stanley* was incredibly hard and Adrian Stalham turned up at exactly the point I needed after a big setback.

His support, guidance and input has been invaluable over the first year and continues to be.

Big thanks to Emma for leaving a great business to follow me; thanks to the growing *S&S* crew – this journey has only just got started; and thanks to Cal for all his work on the book.

A massive thanks to my family for all their support – Mum, Dad, Jenny, Malcolm, Florence and Liz.

And a special mention to my dad – Diarmuid Lynes for supporting this move to create *S&S* and for bringing me on his business journey at an early age.

Your community approach and open nature with people has defined my approach to being at the top of my game in an industry I love.

And most importantly, to my wife for allowing me to put the house and our lives under stress to bring my vision to life. You are a star and none of this would have happened without you, your love and your support.

About the Author

Pat Lynes has been at the top of the IT and change knowledge worker recruitment game for over 15 years and was *Global Interim Recruiter of the Year, 2015.*

He has successfully delivered over 100 transformation teams for the likes of *Burberry, Argos, Sky* and *Everything Everywhere.*

Pat was part of the leadership team that won *Best Company To Work For* and *Fastest Growing Company* in the UK for five consecutive years.

He delivered a seven figure divisional business for a large global technology recruitment company and also recently co-built the largest independent technology and change recruitment company in the UK to an eight figure revenue business within six years.

Visioning a future world for his game he decided to create the challenger brand, *Sullivan & Stanley,* to solve CIOs and boards problems around the widening *capability* and *speed* gap in today's organisations.

Sullivan & Stanley is a premiere top 5% crowd company for executive Interims, the originator of the *Teams as a Service* model and the *Change Society* professional community designed to transform and future-proof companies against disruptive technology.

Pat is married to Helen, with two boys, Sullivan and Stanley.

Contact

To close your capability and speed gap forever, tap into *The Change Society*. Please contact *Sullivan & Stanley* at:

Website	www.sullivanstanley.com
Email	TIR@sullivanstanley.com
LinkedIn	*www.linkedin.com/in/patricklynes/*
YouTube	*Sullivan & Stanley*
Twitter	*@patlynes* and *@sullyandstan*
Facebook	*www.facebook.com/sullivanandstanley/*